Experiencing *Life's* Challenges...
BUT GOD!

IN EVERY TRIAL, TEMPTATION, TEST, AND PROBLEM GOD'S PURPOSE WILL PREVAIL

JACKIE BAILEY-MOORE

Cover Design and drawing: Bobby Parker
Graphics: Steve Jones and Alex Jackson of: Express it! Digital Print Center LLC

Song Lyrics: Found on website

Printed in the United States

Contents

Dedication v

Acknowledgments vii

Foreword.. xiii

Introduction xv

Chapter 1 "Hallelujah Anyhow".. 1

Chapter 2 "He's A Keeper" 37

Chapter 3 "The Prayer of Faith".. 50

Chapter 4 "Out of the Box" 68

Chapter 5 "I'm Grateful" 88

Epilogue 101

But God Scriptures... 107

Dedication

This book is dedicated to the honor and memory
of my late husband Albert Moore Jr.
Thank you for your love, support,
encouragement, prayers, and for pushing me to do my best
in whatever I put my hands, heart, and mind to do.
With your military mindset, you pushed me beyond what I
thought I could do, and this book is evidence of how you never
gave up on me and you didn't allow me to give up on myself.

Love and miss you dearly!

Acknowledgments

First and foremost, I want to thank and praise my Lord and Savior Jesus Christ for equipping and qualifying me to write "BUT GOD." Truly, all the glory, honor, and praise is due Him because I know for a fact that had it not been for Him being who He is in my life which is my everything I could not have done it with my strength. To God be the glory for the great things He has done.

To my Pastor Rev. Dr. Silas M. Townsend and First Lady Deaconess Ida R. Townsend, you already know. The both of you have been there for me through death and sickness and to rejoice with me when I had so much to rejoice about. You encouraged and prayed for me when I felt discouraged. I can't thank you enough for your support, encouraging words, love, and prayers. I am so grateful and appreciative to you both for all that you have done for me and I am so Godly proud to be called your Rev. Daughter! I want the world to know that I have the best Pastor and First Lady on this planet.

To my Mom, Deaconess Christine Bailey, whom I love dearly, without you there would be no me. With everything you've been through since your diagnosis of Colon Cancer in 2010 you have demonstrated to me and our family that: "The Lord is good; His mercy is everlasting, and His truth endureth to all generations" Psalm 100:5.

To my #1Son, Carvin (Cheeks) Bailey, who is the apple of my

eye, bone of my bone and flesh of my flesh. From the very first day that you came into this world not to mention into my life, you have brought me nothing but pure joy. I am so grateful to God for the man of God you have become. Thank you for being such an added blessing by adding your testimony to this book, and thank you for being the encourager you are to me and for speaking Godly wisdom. I love you with my whole heart!

To my cousin who is more like a sister to me, Darella White. You were the very first person whom God allowed me to show this project to in its birthing stage, and you were able to read a portion of the first chapter. I sat and watched your facial expressions while you were reading and really I couldn't tell if you liked it or disliked it! Couldn't tell if you were encouraged or discouraged, but your words of encouragement meant the world to me. Love you dearly and thanking God always for allowing us to be a part of the same family tree (The Bailey's).

To my brother, Charles (Stump) Bailey, and my cousin who is more like my brother, Vincent Graham, I can not thank you enough for always being there for me no matter what and for being the men that our grandfather the late Louis Graham exemplified and instilled in you to be. Both of you hold so many of his qualities but caring and supporting the family is at the top of the list.

To my loving family, the Bailey's, Graham's, Moore's, and Coleman's which are too numerous to name. I cannot begin to thank God enough for each one of you for you all hold a special place in my heart. Thank you for the many times you encouraged me to never give up. I love you all. You are the best!!

To my dear and amazing sister friends, Minister Joann Cade, Gladys Sheppard, and Rev. Bertha Dunlap whom I love dearly and so thankful for your love, encouragement, and prayers. I want you to know how grateful to God I am for each of you and for the special sisterhood we share.

To my Armor Bearer, Addline Spann (aka Bishop), who not only assist me every time I have to go out to spread the gospel but who will and does pray for me every chance she gets. You have been my sounding board when needed and you have always given me Godly wisdom and advice when necessary. Thank you for just being who you are and for being that listening ear I so needed at times.

To my spiritual daughters, Kym Hodges and Deena Williams. There aren't enough words in the English language to express how grateful I am and what I feel in my heart for the both of you. You opened up your heart to what the Lord spoke to your spirit concerning me and this book and I just want to say thank you. Kym, you were the driving force and inspiration the Lord knew I needed to get started and to get the job done. You never gave up on me even when I wanted to give up on myself. Your frequent calls are what inspired me to get the job done. I love you both dearly!

To my Potter's House women, you ladies cannot be compared to. Thanking God always for each one of you. I can't thank God enough for the joy, love, and blessings you bring to me. Each one of you have truly grown spiritually, and for that, I am so grateful. Continue to stand on the promises of God and never stop soaring to higher heights in Him.

My heartfelt thanks to Mr. Bobby Parker who doesn't mind using his gifts and talents to be a blessing to many. Thank you for being an added blessing to this project by using your artistic gift of drawing the picture on the front cover. I thank God for you.

To my St. John Church family in Camden, NJ, the Honeycomb church, where you have done nothing but show me love dripping in honey. You are so incredible and there is none like you. You all have been such a blessing in my life and I just want you to know that I love you all St. John and from my lips to your ears, "You Rock."

In Loving Memory of

Deacon Louis and Deaconess Mollie Graham
My Grand Parents

and

Deaconess Geraldine Harley
My Aunt

You are no longer here with me but in spirit, you
are still the wind beneath my wings.
You loved me unconditionally and I am forever grateful.

Love and miss you so much!

Foreword

Rev. Jackie Bailey-Moore's divinely inspired book will challenge, encourage and strengthen you in the face of life's trials and tribulations. You will become better equipped to handle not only your own personal challenges but also to be a light and strength to those around you. Rather than giving us pat answers to life's challenges this book points us to God and the principles and promises in the Word of God.

It is often in the midst of the storm that not only we find God's amazing grace but we also find some of His greatest works. This leads us to proclaim by faith "But God". Rev. Moore convincingly attests to the truth that the unknown and the uncontrollable often makes us anxious but in Christ there is peace in the midst of life's fiercest storms.

This book helps us to trust God through every challenge through a deep dependence upon God's Word and a deep assurance that He answers prayer. Rev. Moore glorifies God by acknowledging His sovereignty and His goodness in every challenge in this book. She encourages us by demonstrating from the Word of God that God is in control of our lives that He loves us and He works out all of the circumstances of our lives for our good and His glory.

This book is Biblical and challenging with deep faith building insights gleaned from enormous challenges faced by Rev. Moore and members of her family. This timely book calls us to bring all of our needs to Christ so that he can do a mighty work in us and through us. As a result, our lives will glorify God as never before and produce in us a deeper faith in God. This book is an amazing testament to the truth that God is able to bring us through challenges with greater confidence and renewed hope.

Rev. Silas M. Townsend, D. Min.
Pastor of St. John Baptist Church
Camden, NJ

Introduction

On this journey we call life, we can be sure to face many challenges, experience many trials, and weather through many storms that suppress and oppress us. If there is one thing we can count on to be consistent and ongoing, it is trouble. *"Man that is born of a woman is of few days, and full of trouble" (Job 14:1).*

Trouble is one guarantee in life, that no matter how short or long-lived your life is, it is certain that it will consist of much trouble.

There is no getting around it, and we can't flee from it. Trouble is like a plague that spreads fast and furious and it is found everywhere like in our homes, on our jobs, amongst friends, our families, in our neighborhoods, and yes, even in our churches.

When trouble overtakes your life and causes chaos at extreme levels, it reminds me of the cop and robber movies, when the bad guys are held up in abandoned buildings or in a warehouse and the sheriff or detective yells loudly on a bullhorn; "throw down your weapons, come out with your hands up, you're surrounded." Just imagine the opposite; satan, the ultimate bad guy, threatening you on a day to day basis, commanding you to throw down your weapon – (the word of God) come out with your hands up – (feeling defeated) and declaring that you are surrounded – (paralyzed by fear.)

These are the scare tactics he uses to bully you every chance he gets. His main goal is to make you want to quit and throw in the towel. He feels that if he can engulf your life with havoc, drama, issues, addictions, failing health, and bad relationships, then there is nothing left for you to do but to throw up both your hands and surrender. But surrendering and quitting is not an option when you are determined to walk this walk not by what you see and or feel, but rather by who it is you know, believe, and trust.

Despite that it may seem as though God hasn't worked out the situation yet, you must still trust and believe that in His appointed time, He will. When you can't see His hand, that's when you must trust His plan. It is called faith. *Walk by faith but not by sight (2nd Corinthians 5:7).*

It is not an option to give up or quit, even when you feel like the enemy has overtaken you, when you feel like all hope is gone, or when you've fallen into the deepest and darkest pit. The blessed hope that we have is that no matter what we are faced with in life, it's only for a brief moment and in the end, because of Christ, we are more than conquerors.

Satan tries to dress us with his cheap wardrobe made of trouble, confusion, persecution, and abandonment. The problem is we are so conditioned at times that we buy it and put it on with no hesitation. *We are troubled on every side yet not distressed; we are perplexed; but not in despair; persecuted but not forsaken; cast down, but not destroyed (2nd Corinthians 4:8&9).*

For some, this "doom by design" outfit becomes a part of our everyday dress attire. We wake up in the morning, brush our teeth, and choose to put on his tacky uniform by feeding into the lies he fills our heads with due to our lack of faith and the knowledge of what our God can do!

Yes, we have accepted this to be a part of our everyday life. But when will we learn to dress ourselves in the wardrobe that is designed by God, the garment that gives us the victory over the enemy? God's wardrobe for the believer is an entire armor. The Word says, **"Put on the whole armor of God, that ye may be able to stand against the wiles of the devil." (Ephesians 6:11).**

The wardrobe of satan is made of chains and weights that we have most times willingly accepted. They have become a part of our life, dragging them with us to eat, sleep, hang out, and embrace. But these weights are not for us to cuddle up with, they are not for us to break bread with. We must understand that these weights break us and burden us, but they are temporary hindrances that will soon pass away.

Yes! Temporary! Because even hindrances have an expiration date.

They are just little stepping stones that are getting us ready for something greater and they allow others to see the power of God working in our lives. **"For our light affliction, which is but for a moment, worketh for us a far more exceeding and eternal weight of glory; While we look not at the things which are seen, but at the things which are not seen; for the things which are seen are temporal, but the things which are not seen are eternal." (2nd Corinthians 4:17&18).**

There are situations, circumstances, and people that constantly keep weighing us down. They take advantage of us but it's mostly because we allow them to and then we let guilt overtake us if we don't bend over backward to do for them what they want.

For example, some of us are prisoners in our own homes because we have grown folks, who are 30, 40, 50 years old, who just happen to be our sons and daughters still living under our roofs, and not even working in a "pie factory". That basically means they're not paying any bills, eating up your food, running up the water bill, using electricity, and telling you what and what not to do. The bible says: *"For even when we were with you, this we commanded you, that if any would not work, neither should he eat (2nd Thessalonians 3:10).*

Yes, these are the things that we allow to take place in our lives which causes us to be weary, frustrated, aggravated, and suffer from the condition of being sick and tired of being sick and tired.

It is because you have allowed it that you have now become an enabler, their crutch and leaning post, when, in fact, it is not you that they need to be leaning and depending on but rather it is Jesus Christ.

When we interfere with what God's plans are in the lives of our children and loved ones, we're blocking the hand of God as to what it is He wants and needs to do in their lives. Hard times are sure to come and they're going to have to learn how to pray their way through them, and trust God just like we had to do. It didn't destroy us, nor did it kill us.

Our parents prayed for us through most of life's challenges and what it did for us was make us stronger and wiser. So why not take a page from their book and do the same for our children?

There are people in our family, acquaintances, folks on our job and even in our ministries that we, often times, take the weight of their problems on our shoulders thinking, we have the answers to it all instead of directing them to the one who is the answer. When we take on the weight of other people's problems, we're interfering with what God's perfect plan is for them and their situations. God doesn't need our help, it is we who need His help.

We need to get out of God's way, take our hands off the situation, and trust Him to know that if He knew what was best for us (and He did), then certainly He knows what's best for our children.

There comes a time when you must Strip and Commit! Hand it all over to the Lord! Distant yourself from everything and anyone that slows you down, limits you, and becomes burdensome.

Scripture tells us in **(Hebrews 12:1) – "Let us lay aside every weight…"** For the many folks who use us and who call themselves our friends but in reality, they are more like "frenemies"(an enemy disguised as a friend) - lay that weight aside; for the relationships that some of us are in that is one-sided and toxic and you find yourself giving love but never get love in return - lay that weight aside; for the family members who feel that because you're family, blood-related that you're obligated to do for them and they won't hesitate to remind you that blood is thicker than water, laying a guilt trip on you making you feel duty-bound to pick up the ball each and every time they drop it – the devil is a liar, lay that weight aside; spouses that physically and mentally abuse you as well as manipulate you it's time to lay that weight aside.

There are some of you who have been abandoned by your parents, possibly due to a drug or alcohol addiction, or maybe you were put up for adoption; someone has had to go through the system and you had to endure the tyranny of being put in one foster home after another and you feel no one loves or cares for you, but that couldn't be any further from the truth, because God does care and He does love you unconditionally. When laying this weight aside, you have the blessed promise that: *"When my father and my mother forsake me then the Lord will take me up" (Psalm 27:10).* So just lay that weight aside!!!

Often, life's challenges cause us to waiver in our faith. They will have you questioning and doubting God; it will cause you to have anxiety, wondering how much longer will I have to go through what I'm going through? You will even develop a complaining spirit, but every time we go through anything, we ought not to complain but start reflecting on what the word of God has to say.

- Reflect on - **(Psalm 124:1)** – **"That if it had not been for the Lord who was on our side"** – which serves as a reminder that the Eternal God is our help and support and protection!
- Reflect on - **(Joshua 1:5)** – **"There shall not any man be able to stand before thee all the days of thy life; as I was with Moses, so I will be with thee; I will not fail thee, nor forsake thee"** – which gives us peace and comfort in knowing that whatever the situation He will always be there with and for us!
- Reflect on – **(Luke 20:43)** – **"Til I make thine enemies thy foot stool."** – Lets us know that we don't have to worry about our enemies because the plans that God has for them places them under our feet!
- Reflect on – **(Psalm 27:1)** – **"The Lord is my light and my salvation; whom shall I fear? The Lord is the strength of my life; of whom shall I be afraid?** –which emphatically reassures us that we don't have to fear any man!

Every day that we reflect on the word of God, we will find ourselves drawing closer to Him and it will empower, encourage, educate, equip, and embrace us. All we need to do is make the declaration that it is because of the grace and the mercies of God that with everything I've been through, I'M STILL HERE!!!

It is my desire through the reading of this book to encourage you the reader, to take hold of God's word and read it, study it, and more importantly apply it to give yourself a firm foundation on which to stand so to enable you to know and live out all of these truths and promises about our God.

When you do, then it won't matter that you're caught up in a whirlwind of crises or challenges. It won't matter about the storms that try to overtake you. It won't even matter that you're in an ongoing battle with your children, spouse, family members, and friends, and yes, let's not forget the church folks, because you'll have everything you will ever need when you stand on the word of God. So, hold fast to the promises of God because He's a promise keeper, not a promise-breaker.

Stand tough and keep pressing forward, because waiting for you just around the corner is your answer to your life challenges, problems, and troubles. The only requirements necessary is that you have a true and right relationship with God the Father and know HIM well enough to know that HE cannot only see you through, but HE will bring you through and when He does that's the time to declare "BUT GOD!!

CHAPTER

1

"Hallelujah Anyhow"

Consider it pure joy, my brothers, whenever you face trials of many kinds.

JAMES 1:2 (NIV)

"Hallelujah Anyhow" is an expression often used by one of my dear sister-friends Ms. Corrine, proprietor of "Corrine's Place" located here in the city Camden, NJ.

We are both members of St. John Baptist Church and she is a member of the "Potter's House Ministry" of which the Lord has blessed me to be the ministry leader.

I see, talk, and pray with sister Corrine often and whenever I would ask her how she was doing or how were things going with the business, her response to me would be, "sister Jackie, all I can say is "Hallelujah Anyhow." No matter what she was going through, no matter how she was feeling, it was always "Hallelujah Anyhow." You would never catch her complaining about anything and for me as well as the sisters in the ministry, those two words would always be the pick me up that we so needed to hear.

After hearing it for a while, the phrase kind of grew on all of us. It's because of Sister Corrine's conviction of this phrase, that we would always leave her presence feeling that same conviction of knowing that no matter what comes our way, it's "Hallelujah Anyhow."

How many times have you come across someone that every time you had a conversation with them, or just simply ask them how they were doing, their response would always come in the form of a complaint?

You know the kind of folks I'm speaking of. They're the ones that complain so much that at the first sign of seeing them coming, your first instinct is to run in the opposite direction and when you do it gives you a greater appreciation of the movie "Forrest Gump" when Jenny yelled:"Run Forrest, Run."

Too many of us are not happy unless we are complaining. When life isn't turning out the way we thought it should – we complain!

When God doesn't answer our prayers when and how we want Him to – we complain! When the sun shines – we complain that it's too hot and when God sends the rain to cool us down – we complain that the rain is ruining our plans or sisters, we complain about how the rain is going to mess up the hair! Or brothers you complain because you just washed the car. No matter what the situation is we can never be satisfied. We just grumble and complain.

I've realized that it is during these complaining moments, that we need to understand that complainers never win, and complaining never changes much of anything.

It's when we trust that God is in full control of our lives, that He is not a man that He should lie and that whatever He says He will do, He will do it, which should leave no room for us to complain. **"God is not a man that He should lie; neither the son of man, that He** should repent: hath He said, and shall He not do it? Or hath he spoken, and shall He not make it good?" (Numbers 23:19).

Being lied to is the work of satan and he does it well. **"For he is a liar and the father of it" (John 8:44)** and he has no problem in getting us to believe his lies but no matter how many lies he tell it doesn't change the fact that God is still in control of everything that goes on in our lives.

God's word is true and because it is we don't have to be shaken, uprooted, traumatized, victimized, or taken by surprise by anything the adversary says or does because **"Ye are of God, little children, and have overcome them: because greater is He that is in me than he that is in the world" (1ˢᵗ John 4:4).**

There have been times when God brought us out of a whole lot of mess that we got ourselves into, yet we had the audacity to complain forgetting the many, many times that He delivered us; protected us, and provided for us right in the middle of it all.

How quickly we get amnesia after God has been so faithful and merciful to us even when we're being disobedient to Him.

In everything that you may be going through right now don't allow it to cause you to forget all about the impeccable track record that God holds in your life that gives evidence as to what He has already done!

When you give God a "Hallelujah Anyhow" praise, what you are saying to your troubles; what you are confirming with your trials; informing your storms; making clear to your circumstances, and validating to your problems, is that the more you keep showing up at my front door uninvited the more intense my "Hallelujah Anyhow" praise is going to get. You're telling them that even though the heat is on in your life, you're not going to allow yourself to be overtaken or overwhelmed by what comes because you are fully acquainted with and aware as to who it is that's controlling the temperature and His name is Jesus.

The Christian life is not always trouble-free. We still have struggles and hardships and we still have pains and hurts that keep coming. It's a reality and truth that is based on **(Job 14:1) "Man that is born of a woman is of few days, and full of trouble."** This truth lets us know that trouble can and will come at any given time. We don't go looking for trouble, but we can expect it to find us at any place and at any time.

It is because we are Christians; a royal priesthood; and children of the Most High God, that trouble will come unannounced and surround us trying to hold our praise hostage. But there comes a time in our lives when the adversary needs to know that our praise has been held hostage long enough and that nothing and no one will keep you from praising your God.

Trouble is like a magnet to the believer. Its main objective is to latch itself onto you so as to discourage you and draw you away from the will of God. It comes at you like a mighty rushing wind, trying to keep you out-of-focus and have you thrown off course. It is to make you fearful and doubtful. But as long as we stay in the word, believe it, and apply it to our lives, it's not to say that we will be trouble-free, but we will have all of what we need to be able to go through whatever the situation and come out with a "Hallelujah Anyhow praise." **(James 1:22) –"But be ye doers of the word and not hearers only, deceiving your own selves."**

The word of God is the fuel, it is the only true source that we need to face and endure anything that the enemy attacks us with.

It is everything we need for it to be in our lives. It is the light in our darkness; it is the deliverance in our bondage; it is the healing for our mind, body, and soul; it is the comfort in our sorrow; it is the understanding in our confusion; it is the peace in our chaos, and it is the joy in our sadness.

So shall my word be that goeth forth out of my mouth; it shall not return unto me void, but it shall accomplish that which I please, and it shall prosper in the thing whereto I sent it (Isaiah 55:11).

We will never know the true power of God's word and what it can do for us in any given situation until we read it for ourselves, meditate on it, and believe in what it says and what it can do.

When we do as **(2ⁿᵈ Timothy 2:15) says: "Study to shew thyself approved unto God, a workman that needeth not to be ashamed, rightly dividing the word of truth"** and as **(Colossians 3:16) says: "Let the word of Christ dwell in you richly in all wisdom..."** we will witness the true power of Gods Holy word.

The word of God is that beacon of light that we need to light up our path in a dark, mean, and cruel world. **"Thy word is a lamp unto my feet, and a light unto my path." (Psalm 119:105).**

In February 2012, I attended The Bethany Baptist Association School of Biblical Studies for Ordination along with four of my sisters in ministry and upon completion, we had six weeks of Doctrinal Summation, where we had to not only put to memory but have a working knowledge of twelve Articles of Faith.

Article one was of The Scriptures which says:

> *"We believe that the Holy Bible was written by men divinely inspired, and is a perfect treasure of heavenly instruction; that it has God for its author, salvation for its end, and truth without any mixture of error for its matter; that it reveals the principles by which God will judge us, and therefore is, and shall remain to the end of the world, the true center of Christian union, and*

*the supreme standard by which all human conduct,
creeds, and opinion shall be tried."*

In learning, reciting, and memorizing the article of the scrip-tures, some keywords stood out in my mind and it isn't that I didn't already know, but they helped to give me a deeper understanding and a reality check as to just how powerful the word of God truly is and that it will always accomplish what God has purposed it to do: *(1) God is the author, (2) salvation is the end result, (3) it is truth without any error, (4) and it will remain to the end of the world.*

The word of God is pure, holy, right and true. It is the one and only true source that we need to guide us and keep us on the right path in a dark and dismal world.

Many things in life are temporal and will pass away. Friends loved ones and yes even this earth one day, but the word of God is not one of them. It is from everlasting to everlasting. The lies of satan are temporary, but the truth of God's word is eternal.

*Heaven and earth shall pass away:
But my words shall not pass away.
(Mark 13:31)*

*The grass withereth, the flower fadeth:
but the word of our God shall stand
forever. (Isaiah 40:8)*

We serve an Eternal God whose word is Eternal and it will last throughout all eternity.

In the word of God, we can always find an eternal solution for a temporary problem. It can fix whatever is broken; it has the power to open up blinded eyes; it gives you direction when you're lost; put you back on the right path when you've gone astray and it will give you hope when you feel you're at the end of your rope. We must trust and believe that God is able to do just what His word says it will and can do.

> **Trust in the Lord with all thine heart and**
> **lean not unto thine own understanding.**
> **In all thy ways acknowledge him, and he shall**
> **direct thy paths. (Proverbs 3:5&6)**

God's word is "GOD BREATHED." It is the Living Word that enables us to bear witness to so many things that have been manifested in our lives as well as being set free from the bondage of addiction; low-self-esteem; jealousy; rejection; guilt; shame; unforgiveness etc., all because of the true liberating power of the word of God.

We all need to be liberated if not from something then it may be from someone. But whether it is from something or someone the fact remains that all of it is still bondage. The something or someone can repress and oppress you; burden and trouble you. But it is my belief as well as my conviction, based on the word of God that no matter how long people have been oppressed and or in bondage; no matter who it is that's being oppressed, the good news is that God does hear their cries.

They do not go unnoticed and He does not ignore the cries of His people. He may not answer or attend to your cries right away or when you want Him to, but just keep on praying, keep trusting, and I guarantee you that when your answer does come, it will be right on time.

> **"Thou shall neither vex a stranger, nor oppress**
> **him: for ye were strangers in the land of Egypt.**
> **Ye shall not afflict any widow, or fatherless child.**
> **If thou afflict them in any wise, and they cry at**

all unto me, I will surely hear their cry." (Exodus 22:21-22)

Out of their oppression, the Israelites had cried out to God while being in Egypt for over 400 years for deliverance and the fact remains that they cried out to God and God heard their cry; He saw and He knew their pain; and He never forgot His covenant with Abraham, Isaac, and Jacob and so He delivered them.

The same holds true for you and I today! You have been crying out to God for quite some time and haven't gotten an answer nor have you seen any results, but I assure you that God hears, God sees, and God will certainly deliver. He won't fail you or let you down. It will happen but it's going to happen only in God's perfect timing.

I believe God takes great joy and pleasure in delivering His children, but we must learn to wait patiently and understand that He works on a schedule that's not known to man and one that we cannot see nor figure out. The truth of the matter is this, we don't need to know the why's, the when's, and the how comes of the things that happen in our lives or how and when God is going to work it all out we just simply need to know and trust Him.

In the words of Dottie Peoples – "He may not come when you want Him, but He'll be there right on time. He's an on-time God, yes He is."

It is during those trying times when we're waiting to hear from God or waiting to see Him move in our situation that we must learn to do what David did when he was so distressed and when there was talk of stoning him. He encouraged himself in the Lord his God.

"And David was greatly distressed: for the people spoke of stoning him, because the soul of all the people was grieved, every man for his sons and for

his daughters; but David encouraged
himself in the Lord his God."
(1ˢᵗ Samuel 30:6)

It's a real blessing to be encouraged by friends and loved ones when facing adversity, but there will be times in our lives when we will have to encourage ourselves. Encouraging oneself is what we must do to make it through. We must tell ourselves that no matter what, that in every trial, temptation, test, and or problems, God is going to hear our cry. He will show Himself to be faithful and whatever His purposes and His plans are for our lives will prevail.

I have faced many challenges in life, but there is one that stands out over all the rest and it was concerning my husband.

Day 1 – The Challenge Begins

I can remember the time when I had to encourage myself in dealing with some health issues that my husband was going through. It was a situation that called for an "Hallelujah Anyhow."

It was the latter part of March in 1990 on a Saturday evening when my husband and I were sitting in our living room talking, and all of a sudden, he began to look and sound unlike himself. I asked him what was wrong, he replied honey I don't know but I think I need to go to the hospital. For him to suggest that he go to the hospital I knew that something was definitely wrong.

We went to the ER and he was put into a room of which he sat on the side of the bed waiting to be seen. We sat there and we waited, waited and we sat for what felt like a lifetime before anyone attended to him. After a while, he began talking a little out of his head and I became even more troubled and concerned.

In the attempt to go get my husband some help, he made a noise and when I turned to see what the problem was his body slumped over and he began to slide off the bed at which point I rushed out into the hall yelling that someone needs to get in here and see to my husband right now.

Still taking their time, finally, a doctor came strolling in the room and when he saw my husband sliding halfway off the bed he rushed over to him calling for assistance. Before I knew it nurses and doctors were coming from everywhere and machines were quickly being brought into the room.

Everything at this point was moving so quickly that it was making my head spin. They began pushing me to the side to get to him all the while, trying to get some answers, I began screaming what is wrong with my husband? What is happening to him? Very abruptly they asked me to step outside the room and they shut the door.

There I was standing in the hall staring at a closed-door not knowing what was going on, on the other side of it, and not knowing what to do to help my husband. I can't ever remember feeling so helpless. The time will come if it hasn't already when you find yourself in a crisis asking the question, "What do you do when you don't know what to do?" Well, the only thing we can do is pray and stand! We are reminded in **Ephesians 6:13: "Wherefore take unto you the whole armour of God, that ye may be able to withstand in the evil day, and having done all, to stand."**

I was standing, yes, but not in my own strength, but in the power and the strength of Almighty God. One thing that I've learned for certain, is that it matters how we respond when we're in the midst of or going through crisis because it will determine just how well we will be able to stand through it all. All I knew was that there wasn't any more movement, I didn't hear anyone talking and I didn't see a doctor or a nurse for what seem to be forever.

Standing there all alone, with no one to talk to; with no one to encourage or to reassure me that everything was going to be alright I started rubbing and wringing my hands and I began encouraging myself: "Jackie, you don't need to worry! God healed him before and He can do it again! Put your faith into action, Jackie, and trust God with everything that's in you" is what I told myself.

Well, as a child I was brought up on the hymns of the church and while I was pacing back and forth in front of that closed door with my hands clasped one of my favorite hymns came up in my spirit which was "Just a Little Talk With Jesus" and the chorus to that song is: **"Now let us have a little talk with Jesus, let us, tell Him all about our troubles, He will hear our faintest cry and He will answer by and by, now when, you feel a little prayer wheel turning, and you know a little fire is burning, you will find a little talk with Jesus makes it right."**

Talking to Jesus is exactly what I did. I began asking Him to work this situation out for Al's good. I asked Him to heal his body and for Him to be the attending physician in that room. I trust You, Lord, and I believe every word when it says: **"But He was wounded for our transgressions, he was bruised for our iniquities: the chastisement of our peace was upon him, and with his stripes, we are healed" (Isaiah 53:5).** I'm crying out to You, Lord, on Al's behalf, knowing that you hear my cry and believing that you can and you will heal him and see him through this ordeal.

Well, not long after that talk with Jesus, the door flew wide open, wide enough for me to see them putting the defibrillator on Al at which time he sat straight up with his eyes stretched wide open and then immediately he laid back down and quickly once again the door shut.

A few minutes later, one of the doctors came out and approached me to say: Mrs. Moore, I'm sorry but I believe you need to call your priest because it doesn't look like your husband is going to make it. At that moment, everything in me wanted to scream, "what do you mean he's not going to make it??? but I didn't because the spirit of God wouldn't let me and He reminded me in that instant that **"Greater is he that is in me, than he that is in the world" (1ˢᵗ John 4:4).**

The talk that I just had with Jesus was so timely and it was what I needed to calm my spirit to prepare me to process what this doctor just said to me. But because of the omnipresence of God, there was no need for me to process anything simply because I believed with everything in me, that He was already in control. He was already taking care of business and because He was, with Holy Ghost boldness I was able to respond to that doctor by saying: My husband and I walked into this hospital and just like we walked in, I'm believing by faith that by my God's grace He's going to allow him to walk out.

My next statement to him was: "I don't have a priest as you know it, but I do have a High Priest named Jesus and I've already talked with Him now I need to call my Pastor.

It was then that the door opened once more and there my Al was with tubes running everywhere. When I saw him in the state he was in I just froze.

I couldn't believe what my eyes were seeing. It was almost impossible to see him due to all the tubes and machines that they had hooked up to him.

I followed behind the stretcher as they took him to ICU and while walking behind them, I was asking where I could go to use the phone?

While they were getting Al situated I called my Pastor, Rev. Dr., Silas M. Townsend and I began telling him about Al and he assured me that he would be right there.

I knew my God was with me because after seeing my husband with all of those tubes and machines hooked up to him, I was still somewhat calm and I didn't totally lose it. All I could do was keep trusting and believing that God was going to see him through this as well as myself.

It wasn't too long before my Pastor showed up being the encourager that he always is and the prayer he prayed for Al was so powerful that I felt in my spirit that it moved the mountain of Al's sickness and that my husband was already healed.

When you have a Pastor of whom you can call and depend on and who does exactly what he says he's going to do, you are truly blessed. A Pastor who very rarely sends anyone in his place to see about his sheep and will always show up when called upon. A Pastor who has a genuine love for his people and knows every member by name. A Pastor for which I'm grateful for and thank God for each and every day.

The Lord was making it so clear to me that He was in full control of Al's situation down to who his doctors were. Starting with Dr. Brooks, who was his primary doctor (whom I called Moses) and Dr., Rhymes, who happened to be one of his attending Physicians in the hospital (whom I called Joshua). Much to my surprise, Dr. Rhymes and I had attended class together for Biblical Studies at which time I did not know that he was a Medical Doctor, so when I saw him at the hospital I was done. All I could say was WOW GOD!! WOW!!!

What a blessing it was that I personally knew both doctors attending to my husband and they were saved!!! Yes, Lord, Yes!!!

Each day that Al was in the hospital they were full of tests, trials, problems, and challenges that were becoming a little hard for me to deal with, but what was hard for me, I knew it wasn't hard for my God. I knew He could handle, fix, and work it all out. For you see, I was reminded of the written word that says: **"Ah Lord God! Behold, thou hast made the heaven and the earth by thy great power and stretched out arm, and there is nothing too hard for thee" (Jeremiah 32:17)** and also **(Luke 18:27)" And he said, the things which are impossible with men are possible with God."**

Day 2 – Test Of Obedience!

The second day of testing which was on Sunday, started with fluid building up in Al's body causing him to swell up so much that you almost couldn't recognize him. He was out of it and he knew nothing about what was going on with him. He was just lying there not responding to anything or anyone. But through it all by faith, I kept on trusting and believing that God was going to heal him.

I had so much trust and faith in God for Al's healing that I found myself praying and believing God not only for him but also for those who were sick around him. I put Al into the hands of God and I completely trusted Him with what was going on with his condition.

Once I did that, I felt a strong need to pray for those who were sick in the beds all around Al.

What I was feeling was so overwhelming. I felt the spirit of God moving me into obedience to do what He was instructing me to do in that hospital.

Yes, I was there every day and night seeing to my husband, but there were other issues going on around him that God wanted me to see.

There was a young lady in the bed next to Al and there was a young man who was there by her side every day. I asked him what's wrong with her and he said she was in a coma. I asked would he mind if I prayed for her and he replied no I don't mind.

Just before I got ready to pray, two deacons from my church showed up to visit with Al the now late Deacon Ray and the late Deacon Satchel.

I asked them to come and pray with me for this young girl and they did. That was a James 5:14 moment: **"Is any sick among you? let him call for the elders of the church; and let them pray over him, anointing him with oil in the name of the Lord."** We anointed her and prayed over her. Afterward, they visited and prayed with Al and then they left.

I then went to the bedside of a man who was across from Al who also had a lot of machines and tubes running everywhere. There wasn't anyone there with him and so I went in his room read scripture, held his hand, and prayed for him.

On my way back to the bedside of my husband, I looked over and there was a lady who was in the bed on the other side of him. I did not know what was wrong with her but whatever her sickness was I was trusting and believing that God would work it out and so I began praying for her. Before praying I read scripture over her.

One thing that I've learned during this faith walk is that when you're obedient to doing the will of our Father He will be faithful in handling the affairs of His children.

I then left her bedside and I returned to my husband and began praying again for him. Right after praying with him a Doctor approached me and asked if I was Mrs. Moore and I said yes. He told me his name and then he proceeded to tell me that he was my husband's kidney doctor and that my husband was 'really' sick. I stopped him and asked if we could please step away from my husband's bedside so that he could give me any report that he had.

My sole purpose for asking him to do that was because I know that words have power and even though Al wasn't being responsive, I truly believed that he could still hear what was going on and being said around him and I felt he didn't need to hear anything negative concerning his condition. At that moment, I was reminded of what the word of God says that: **"Death and life are in the power of the tongue" (Proverbs 18:21a)** and because I know that words matter and I wasn't allowing him to speak negatively.

He ignored my request and kept trying to tell me how sick Al was and again I insisted that we step away from his bed.

Finally, he did what I asked but very snappishly he says, I only came to let you know that your husband's kidneys are failing and he is 'really' sick. I thanked him for his report and he left.

I truly felt the enemy was using this doctor to set me up to fail and to cause me to act unseemly since I was obedient in praying for the sick that was around my husband. But then again, I thought, this could very well be a test from God so that His glory would be revealed through me. So immediately I just began thanking my God for not letting me become someone else other than whom I proclaim to be, which is saved, born again, and a child of the King.

The hour had gotten really late and one of the nurses asked me if there was something that she could do for me or if I needed anything. I replied yes! The only thing I need is a room where I can rest and pray. She took me to a little room that wasn't too far from ICU.

During the night, I would go back and forth from the room to Al's bedside, laying hands, praying, and thanking God that here it is day 2 and he's still here. This is one of those times where I found myself literally doing as the scripture instructs us to do, **"Pray without ceasing. In everything give thanks: for this is the will of God in Christ Jesus concerning you" (2ⁿᵈ Thessalonians 5:17&18).**

Day 3 – Still Trying To Respond And Not React!

Early Monday morning as I was going to check on Al, I met another doctor who approached me in the same like manner as the previous doctor. She asked if I were Mrs. Moore, and I said yes. She then told me her name and that I'm your husband's liver doctor and I just wanted you to know, at this time, I interrupted her and asked if we could step away from Al's bed before she gave me the report.

She was being very persistent in giving me her report but then again so was I. Trying to respond in a Christ-like manner and not react unseemly, again, I asked that we step away. Very reluctantly, she did as I asked her to do and she proceeded to give me the report that your husband's liver is failing and that he was very sick.

I thanked her for the report and as I turned away from her to go back to my husband's bedside, low and behold another Doctor started walking towards me. By now I was a little tired of how I was being approached by these doctors but as tired as I was, I was able to recognize that what was happening was nothing more than an attack of the adversary.

In my spirit, I began talking to the Lord asking Him to help me to respond to this doctor in a Christ-like manner and not react to anything that he says or does. As he got close to me his approach was not as the other two doctors as He didn't ask if I were Mrs. Moore. With what I felt to be a little sarcastic his words to me were: "You must be Mrs. Moore," which let me know that he must have had a conversation with the other two doctors about me. My response to him was, yes that I am and whom might you be? He gave me his name and never taken a breath he said you know, at this time, I stopped him and told him that if you already know my name, it lets me know that you must have consulted with the other two Doctors who came before you and I'm so sure they told you what my request is and if you cannot honor my request then I would ask that you do not say anything else and I will gladly ask to speak with another doctor.

He stepped away and again being very cynical he said, "Well, I just came to tell you that your husband is a very sick man and the only organ that seems to be functioning normally right now is his heart." I looked that doctor in the eye and all I could say was "Hallelujah thank You Jesus" which was my "in everything give thanks and praise." It was my "Hallelujah Anyhow praise." He looked at me as if to say this woman has bumped her head. I thanked him for the report and proceeded to let him know that the report you just gave me was a good report, because my husband had a heart attack a few years prior and for it to be the only organ functioning normally lets me know that my God is still at work. With a little attitude, he walked away. Oh well!!!

When I married my husband, I became what the Bible says I am his helpmate and so as his wife I was doing for him what Al couldn't do for himself which was speak up for him. But in addition to that, I also became his covering. I covered him in prayer and I made sure that no negative talk would take place around him even if it was the doctors bringing their reports.

Later that evening, my sister–friend, Rev. BJ Torres, came to visit Al. It's nothing like having a sister-friend on whom you can call on at any time and without hesitation, she's right there praying with you and for you. I shared with her everything that was going on with him and how the doctors were coming with their reports.

He was not passing any water and based on the reports given to me from the doctors regarding his kidneys and liver failing I knew I had to keep praying, I knew I had to keep trusting and believing in my God.

This was not the time for me to go into panic and stress mode. No, I had to stay in faith mode. I had to keep **"walking by faith and not by sight" (2ⁿᵈ Corinthians 5:7).**

Through my natural eyes, things weren't looking good for Al, but through the eyes of God, his situation was right where I felt God needed it to be so that He and He alone might get all the Glory and that the doctors would get to know who the true physician in Al Moore's case really was.

In seeing through God's eyes, it also served as a reminder to me as to how great and faithful He is. No matter how bad a situation may look to you through your own eyes always remember that the same situation through the eyes of God, is right where it needs to be so that when He brings you out of it, man will unequivocally know and get to see firsthand the awesome power of a Sovereign God who does His best work in bad situations that don't look good and seemingly don't give us much hope.

While I was pondering over and over again in my mind everything that Al was going through, I focused on the obvious which was the swelling in his body because I felt that if the fluid didn't come out of him, it could build up around his heart you remember (the only organ that was functioning normally).

What I felt I needed to do was to be specific in my praying and ask God to allow Al to pass that water. All I knew was that my husband needed a special touch that only God could give.

My sister BJ stayed at the hospital with me that night and in that little room that was given me, we both began to pray. **"For where two or three are gathered in my name, there am I in the midst of them" (Matthew 18:20)** My prayer was, God, Al needs you, I need you. You know all about the reports that were given me concerning his condition, but your word asks the question: "whose report will you believe?" and God I choose to believe the report of the Lord. After praying, I had such a peace and calm that I rested in the Lord and I fell asleep.

Day 4 – It's Morning!

As Tuesday morning quickly approached which was the fourth day of Al's ordeal, I woke up being hopeful for a move from God. I went to check on him and as I looked down on him, I saw a ray of hope. I saw what seemed for me to be a sign of answered prayer.

I saw the catheter bag hanging at the foot of his bed whereas for the past three days was empty, it was bone dry because he had not passed any water. But early Tuesday morning as I continued to stare at that bag, I thought my eyes were playing tricks on me; I thought I wasn't seeing clearly, but there was nothing wrong with my eyes and I was seeing very clearly. It was no mistake that I saw a small drop of water fall into that bag. Yes, I said a small drop!!!! **(Lamentations 3:21) "This I recall to my mind, therefore have I hope."**

God showed me a sign of what I knew to be the beginning of my prayers being answered. Now for some that one small drop may not have been enough to get excited over or to get one's hopes up but for me, it was more than enough evidence to assure me that everything was going to be alright. It was more than enough proof for me to know that God was at work.

There will be times in our lives when we won't be able to see the hand of God working at all and then again there might be times when we may be blessed to get a small glimpse of what God is doing to work out the situation. But whether you see or don't see His hand at work you can always trust His plan, which very well may consist of small steps.

Everything God does in us and for us in life does not always start out on a grand scale, but we can trust that His way of doing anything in our lives is right and good. Don't lose hope, don't be discouraged when things don't seem to be working out the way you think they should or if the steps it takes to get you to your destiny doesn't start with a big bang, but rather be encouraged by the portion of scripture that says: **"Do not despise these small beginnings"** (Zechariah 4:10) NLT.

We should never look down on or frown upon anything in our lives that might start out small as opposed to starting out on a large grand scale because it doesn't really matter how small your dreams, aspirations, and visions may start out to be, just trust God with it and watch how little will become much when you put it all in the Master's hand. Be thankful and appreciative of every little thing in life with the understanding that our God is the God of little things as well as all big things.

In our frustration, we allow ourselves to be distracted by the small things happening around us, but many times our greatest blessings are found and wrapped up in the small things. Paul tells us in **(1st Thessalonians 5:18:) "In everything give thanks: for this is the will of God in Christ Jesus concerning you."** We are so focused on the big picture, that we forget to thank Him for the small things that it took to get us there. So, when thanking Him, start by thanking Him for all the little things we seemingly take for granted. Thank Him for waking you up this morning; thank Him for life health and strength; thank Him for being in your right mind; thank Him for your salvation.

For God to allow me to see that small drop in that big bag I believe was His way of letting me know that as long as I stay focused on Him and not the circumstances that try to distract me, my small beginnings will suddenly and supernaturally end up with big results.

When I prayed that specific prayer, I prayed it with a thankful heart and the belief that God would hear and answer my prayer. I didn't pray amiss, I didn't pray in doubt nor did I waver. No, I prayed and believed by faith. I prayed, believing His word that says: **"And this is the confidence that we have in him, that if we ask anything according to his will, he heareth us: And if we know that he hear us, whatsoever we ask, we know that we have the petitions that we desired of him."(1st John5:14-15).**

When we are certain that God hears our prayers and also trust and believe that He not only hears us when we pray but that He truly listens as well, we can have that blessed assurance that our prayers are already answered and that whatever we ask of Him by faith, we already have it. **"I will answer them before they even call me.**

While they are still talking about their needs, I will go ahead and answer their prayers! (Isaiah 65:20) NLT.

Our God is a sovereign God who does exactly what He wants. Yes, He does answer our prayers but it's not because we tell Him how and when. Prayers are answered when and however God sees fit. Often, we get impatient and we don't want to wait on God instead we want to hurry God and tell Him what to do. We just have to learn how to trust and wait for His perfect timing because His time is always the right time.

There are times in our prayer life when frustration kicks in but even when it does we should never forget what our role and our place is.

We should never forget that God is the potter and that we are the clay. We should never forget that He is the sovereign one and we are to be the obedient one. I say this because at times, out of desperation, we can find ourselves telling God what we want and demand that He gives it to us when we want it instead of Him telling us what He wants for us and waiting for His timing to get it.

God is a prayer-answering God, but He has His own time table as to when and how our prayers get answered. No matter how long it takes, no matter what detours we must make or what storms may overtake us in the process we must wait on Him for the answer and stop trying to take matters into our own hands.

We must be prayerful and keep on trusting God in everything because the adversary is always on his job trying to distract us from the things of God. He's a negative force who's always bringing negativity into our lives and who wants to have us thinking negatively about everything that God is doing in us and for us. But I truly believe that for every negative that the enemy tries to challenge, distract and discourage us with, God always has a positive that will not only stop and block him but it will show him that God always has the last move and final say concerning each of us.

Day 5 – Afternoon!

After receiving all the negative reports, it was later on in the day on that Wednesday afternoon when God started making another move.

Dr. Rhymes showed up at Al's bedside and he said to me, Sis, I'm here to discuss your husband's condition with you but I need you to know that as his doctor, I have an obligation to give you the medical report of what's going on with him but we both know who's in control and that was music to my ears.

We stepped away from Al's bedside (without me having to ask him) and he told me what was told to me by the other doctors that Al was very sick and that his vital organs were failing.

He preceded to tell me that it was a great possibility that if he were to come out of this, he might have some memory loss. But then he said as your brother in Christ and a man of faith, I have yet another report to give you and that report says that by His stripes he is healed. ("**But he was wounded for our transgressions, he was bruised for our iniquities: the chastisement of our peace was upon him, and with his stripes, we are healed**") Isaiah 53:5.

He then said to me that medically it doesn't look good for him but you and I are not looking at what it looks like but rather at what the word of God has to say about his condition. Now, Sis, he said, whose report do you believe? and without any hesitation, I responded by saying I choose to believe the report of the Lord.

You may be facing a crisis right now where you have received nothing but negative reports. You've gotten a negative report about your health, your children, your spouse, siblings, and even your job but understand this that the negative always shows up before the development of the positive.

It's just like when you take a picture, it first appears as a negative image and to view that negative image clearly, the photographic film and paper have to be treated to produce a positive image of the picture taken. In most situations, they sometimes get worse before they get better but just hold on and hold on until your change comes.

For every negative that the enemy tries to challenge and discourage us with, God always has a positive, not to mention the last move. So let me suggest that you take whatever negative report you may have been given, treat it with the word of God and watch how He will develop a positive report out of a negative situation on your behalf.

Day 5 – Evening - The breakthrough!

Later on that evening, a few of the deacons along with some of the members from my church came to visit Al. It was so many of them that we had to go to the waiting room because Al was still in ICU. While there, we prayed, read scripture, and believed God for a miraculous breakthrough.

They stayed with me for a good while and we talked, laughed, and had a wonderful fellowship. Their visit really helped to ease my mind of what was going on with Al.

The sitting space in that waiting room was very limited and I ended up sitting on top of a desk, which was right next to the door. While sitting there all of a sudden, I turned and when I looked, there stood Dr. Rhymes and I asked him, Doc why are you still here? You're usually gone by now. He responded and said, sis, I was in my car on my way home and the news that I had to give you I was going to give it to you tomorrow, but the Holy Spirit told me to come back and give it to you now.

I asked him what news and he said your husband is showing

miraculous improvement. His kidneys and his liver are functioning at their normal capacity. I leaped off that desk embraced Dr. Rhymes, thanked him for the news, and began thanking and praising my God for his faithfulness in answering our prayers.

I thanked Him for being a God of "suddenly." A God who moves swiftly, surprisingly, and 'totally' unexpectedly. It was at that moment when I realized that it does not take God all day and all night to do anything.

The praise that was coming from that waiting room was enough to get us all put out of the hospital, but we didn't think about that. All we knew was that the prayers went forth on Al's behalf and God answered those prayers "suddenly" Prayers of great faith had gone forth with much power which showed to be effective and exhibited the evidence of God's Holy word written in **(James 5:16b) "The effectual fervent prayer of the righteous availeth much."**

Day 6 – Thursday Morning!

Everyday, starting with the first day of Al's admittance into the hospital, God was doing something to show Himself to be faithful and Sovereign.

Still staying in the room that was provided for me at the hospital, I woke up Thursday morning and after coming out of prayer, I did what I had been doing for the past 5 days and that was to walk over to Al's bedside but this time it wasn't to check on him it was more so to see with great anticipation what move God was going to make next.

To my natural eyes, it did not look like anything had changed outwardly because there he was still lying swollen from head to toe with the same tubes running everywhere and the bag to the catheter still had only that one drop. But all was still well with my soul because even though Al's condition seemed to be the same, I believed that God had a sudden move to make and that supernaturally things were about to change.

A Change has come!

After visiting with Al, I left to go home to shower and to get something to eat. While at home, I received a phone call from Al's brother Sherman who lives in Boston. He called to check on him and to let me know that he was flying in on that Friday to see him. After talking with Sherman, I returned to the hospital and after getting there and once I exited the elevator, I started walking down the hall towards the ICU. While walking the hall Al's bed was in view and I noticed that the curtains were pulled around his bed.

In my mind, I'm wondering, what's going on? did something happen while I was gone? But the closer I got to his bed I could see under the curtain the feet of someone sitting in a chair. Someone was visiting with Al and I soon found out that it was my sister-in-law Georgia and all of sudden she jumped up and abruptly pulled back the curtain and ran from behind it with a strange look on her face. As she ran from behind the curtain, she ran right into me.

I asked her what was wrong and her reply to me was "Girl" that Al is too much and I asked her what happened? her exact words to me were "he done peed so much that he filled up the bag and it's now running all over the floor." All I could say was Hallelujah, thank you Jesus. I then told her, "I don't care if they got to get a paddle and a boat, let it overflow Jesus, just let it overflow."

Here was my answer to a specific prayer, which undoubtedly had a supernatural result that only a supernatural God could give. I specifically asked God for a special touch so that Al would pass that water and God heard and answered my prayers and this was just another time that His glory was being revealed.

I then went to his bedside to witness this great move that only a great God could have done. There he was still lying with the tubes still covering him, but I looked beyond those tubes and I looked at my husband and I just couldn't stop thanking my God for what my eyes were seeing. My Al-boogie as I always call him was beginning to look like himself. The swelling had begun to go down. What started to be a ray of hope with one small drop of water ended up with a miraculous move of God by opening up the flood gates of heaven.

Day 7 – Friday morning/ Al's Birthday!

The day started like every other day while at the hospital with me waking up going into prayer for Al and walking over to his bedside to check on him. But this particular day was very special as it was Al's birthday.

Once I got to his bedside, I leaned over rubbing his forehead, and began singing happy birthday to him.

While sitting with Al, my mother Deaconess Chris Bailey came to see him. As we were talking, I told her that today was going to be a busy day and that because I had been staying at the hospital I wasn't able to do any cleaning or food shopping which had to be done because Al's brother Sherman was flying in and I had to pick him up from the airport.

Being the mother that she is my mom said she would clean my apartment, which would be a big help and all I would have to do was pick up a few things from the supermarket. Oh, what a blessing it was to have my mom there for me as she always is. Talk about being grateful.

We both left the hospital and went to my apartment. I showered got a little something to eat and afterward, I left out to go food shopping. When I got back it was close to the time for me to go pick up my brother-in-law. I put the food away and off to the airport I went.

Friday afternoon - God's completed work!

I picked up Sherman and took him to the apartment to get some-thing to eat. Afterward, we headed straight to the hospital. While on our way I wanted to prepare him for all of the tubes that he would see connected to Al and that he was still unresponsive. He said to me wow, I didn't realize he was that sick. I said yes, he's been going through a pretty rough time, but each day God has been showing himself faithful by making some miraculous moves.

Once we made it to the hospital, we got on the elevator going up to ICU. When getting off the elevator we started walking down the hall and I could see from a distance that something was a little off.

I told Sherman that the bed down there where the curtain was partially drawn, is where Al's bed was. They must have moved him. He asked me why did I think they moved him? I told him because that bed has a TV at the foot of it and he's still connected to a lot of tubes and not responsive.

I said to Sherman let's go over to the desk so I can find out where they moved him because I know that can't be his bed with a TV. As we were walking over to the desk I happened to look over at the bed that the gentleman was in of whom I prayed for and who was covered with tubes as well when Al was first brought to ICU and I saw that he wasn't there. When I saw that his bed was empty, I got 'really' concerned and asked the nurse what happened to the man who was in that bed? She responded by saying oh, he's made some great improvement and he's been moved to a regular floor. All I could say was my God thank you.

I then glanced over at the bed where the young lady who was in a coma was and of whom Deacon Ray, Deacon Satchel, and myself prayed for. Her curtain was drawn around her bed as well, but I heard some voices and suddenly the young man who was there by her bed-side from day to day came from behind the curtain and I asked him how she was doing? he told me to see for myself and low and behold he pulled back the curtain and she was awake and talking.

By this time I know my brother-in-law must have been wondering, when am I going to see my brother, but I just had to know about the lady who was in the bed on the other side of Al of whom I found out later that she had brain surgery. I asked the nurse about her. She said her surgery went well and she too was taken to a regular room.

You can't tell me that God won't show Himself to be faithful.

Once I received the reports of those three patients, I then asked the nurse, where did they move my husband? because where his bed was, I see a TV at the foot of it. She looked at me with the most puzzling look and said Mrs. Moore we didn't move him he's where he's always been. That is his bed.

Before I could say another word, she was answering the phone, so Sherman and I walked down to his bed and when we got there I pulled back the curtain and what my eyes beheld next was nothing short of a miraculous supernatural, sovereign move of a great big wonderful God.

You see, when I left the hospital that morning, my husband was still unresponsive and he was still attached to tubes that covered him from head to toe. BUT GOD!! When I returned and went to his bedside my Al-boogie was sitting up with only one tube on him which was oxygen and he was watching the TV that I couldn't believe was there in the first place.

Standing there in such amazement with tears of great joy, I looked at him and he stared back at me not saying a word. At that moment it suddenly came to my mind what Dr. Rhymes told me that "if he comes out of this there may be a possibility that he will have some memory loss". Well, there was only one way to find that out so with his brother Sherman standing at the foot of the bed, I asked Al did he know who he was and slowly turning his head to look at him with a deep and very raspy voice he started speaking at a snail's pace and said, "He's a Moore" and I said yes he is Al-boogie, yes he is and that answer was good enough for me.

When God does what we ask of Him by faith, He completes and perfects it and He does it in such a way that it is mind-blowing leaving no stone unturned. **"Being confident of this very thing, that he which hath begun a good work in you will perform it until the day of Jesus Christ" (Philippians 1:6).**

When we stay focused on what He wants us to do and not so much on what we want Him to do for us our situation goes from zero to a hundred at the blink of an eye.

Spiritually we know that the number seven means completeness and perfection and on this seventh day of Al's journey God's work was complete. Not only for him but also for the other three patients as well.

Day 8 – Saturday - All Glory goes to God!

Saturday morning, I went to go visit my husband and after being there a while, I told him I was going to the cafeteria to get something to eat and that I would be right back. When I returned a lady from housekeeping was there cleaning and while she was cleaning I over-heard her say to my husband, "Well Mr. Moore, the doctors really worked on you and got you well," and before I knew it I responded by letting her know that undoubtedly and without question, that my husband's healing was miraculous.

It was a miracle, that only my God could do. I proceeded to tell her that yes, the doctors did what they did best and that was to bring me every negative report that they could bring me, but it was my God who turned every negative report into a positive result.

Every doctor that approached me gave me nothing but negative reports with no hope except for Dr. Rhymes. Even from day one when Al was admitted and the doctor told me my husband wasn't going to make it I knew then on whom I was going to have to depend on to be my husband's physician and His name is Jesus. So please I don't mean any disrespect but in the case of Albert Moore all the glory all the honor and all the praise goes to God my Heavenly Father.!

I never quite understood until that moment why I had to be the only one who knew all of what was happening with Al. Why I had to go through all that I went through with him especially when having to deal with the negative reports from the doctors. God did not even allow Al to remember anything of what he went through which means he was not able to tell his own story. I can only surmise that I was the one who needed to remember because I believe God knew that I would tell it. He knew me well enough to know that no matter where I was, whom I was with, and no matter what was going on around me, I would tell the story of God's greatness and His healing power so that when somebody else goes through such an ordeal as this I will be able to tell the story with much conviction and evidence as to how God can and will heal even when the odds are stacked against you. Even when the doctor says no, God's grace and mercy will step right in and say yes.

I can tell the story of how we can not walk by what the situation looks like but rather by what and of whom we believe. Because of this situation, I have become a bona fide witness that if He did it before He can do it again. Just have faith, trust in your God, watch Him move, and then go tell your story that I've seen Him do it.

We all have a plan that God has strategically put in place for each of us that we know not where those plans will lead us, but God is a good and faithful God and His plans for us will not take us where His grace and his mercy will not keep us.

"For I know the plans I have for you, declares the
Lord, plans to prosper you and not to
Harm you, plans to give you hope and a future."
Jeremiah 29:11 NIV

I often use this passage of scripture when extending an invitation to salvation. It's to let one know that God has a purpose and a plan for your life, but so that His plans might come into fruition and become a reality in our lives, we've got to follow His lead, adhere to His instructions, trust Him and be obedient so to be on the right path, going in the right direction, doing what He has called us to do.

God knew the plans He had for me in that hospital, but it was up to me to be obedient so that His purpose and plans would come to fruition. Not just for Al but for all of those He had me praying for.

In any crisis, we have got to let God's will be done at all times. We have got to surrender our will to His will along with our heart, mind, body, and soul.

Give God something to work with and you will soon see your destiny coming into view. What appears to be afar off in the distance will soon be up close and personal. So do not lose hope, encourage yourself, and surrender your all to the Master.

In the words of that great hymn of the church: *"All to Jesus, I surrender, All to Him I freely give; I will ever love and trust Him, In His presence daily live. I surrender all, I surrender all, all to Thee my blessed Savior, I surrender all."*

No matter what ditches have been set up for you; no matter what evil has been spoken about you and no matter what obstacles you find waiting and lurking around the corner; you can be rest assured that they are not a permanent fixture in your life; and they are not here to stay always. Yes, they play a part in our lives, but the part they play often drive us to our knees, and to stay in our word drawing us closer to God. They play a part in our lives that will only last for a season. There's a time and season for everything:

> *"To everything, there is a season, and a time to*
> *Every purpose under the heaven...*
> *(Ecclesiastes 3:1)*

When these obstacles come upon us, we should recognize and know it to be the trick of the enemy to ruffle our feathers and to bring us into that place of frustration, anxiety, and sometimes even doubt and fear.

They are to drive us into having a giving up and quitting spirit, to feel defeated. But there is only one who is defeated and he was defeated over two thousand years ago and here it is two thousand years later and he's still defeated. Then again on the flip side, everything isn't always coming at us from the devil. There will be times when we are tested by God and the test He gives will reveal to us all that we have within us to endure. Being tested is part of the process to help us to reach our destiny and to receive and do all that He has set our hearts, hands, and minds to do for His Glory and the upbuilding of His Kingdom.

Going through the process is part of the course because it is during the process that we grow, mature, and gain wisdom.

It is through the process that when we go through the test without murmuring or complaining; when we go through not being frustrated, agitated, or aggravated; when we go through praising and lifting our hands in total praise, then God will get all the glory; those around us will be blessed, healed, delivered and set free and we will have the victory. Stuff is always happening and it always will but the good news is this, that when it comes, it cannot, nor will it last forever, for this too shall pass.

So even when bad things happen in our lives and they will! Even when things do not go the way we plan and they sometimes won't! Even when things do not make sense and most times they don't! and even when you find yourself getting one bad report after another all we have to do is reflect on what God has already done, remember the when's and the how's of God as to how He brought you out before! How He healed your body before! How He protected you from danger seen and unseen before and shout, "HALLELUJAH ANYHOW"!

A "Hallelujah Anyhow Praise" will not prevent the trials, stop sickness, nor will it block the storms and trouble from coming your way, but this one thing I do know, it will definitely help see you through to a victorious end.

PRAYER OF ENCOURAGEMENT...

Lord, I encourage myself to let go of my will and surrender
it to what your perfect will is for my life. In
every situation and circumstance
I found myself in it was more important for me to know and
remember who you are and what you've already done.
I understand that you are God and God alone and that you
are in complete control and no matter
what happens I will rejoice and
shout -"Hallelujah Anyhow" Amen!

SONG OF ENCOURAGEMENT
"HALLELUJAH ANYHOW"

Hallelujah anyhow.
Never, never let your problems get you down.
When life's problems come your way
Hold your head up high and say
Hallelujah anyhow!

I remember the day remember the hour
God saved me with His Holy Ghost power
Wish you could have been there when I came through
The church was on fire with the Holy Ghost too
I know for myself that I been saved
The angels in heaven done signed my name.
Hallelujah Anyhow!!

You can talk about me just as much as you please

The more you talk I'm gone stay on my knees

I'm on my way up and I ain't gone come down

I'm on my way up to a higher ground

The Lord has been mighty good to me

That's why I'm grateful so grateful to thee

Hallelujah Anyhow!!

Sung by: Creflo Dollar

CHAPTER

2

"He's A Keeper"

The Lord is thy keeper: the Lord is thy
shade upon thy right hand

(PSALM 121:5)

There are many uncertainties in life that will have you not knowing what to expect from one day to another.

With the many conflicts and struggles that often make us feel like our backs are pinned up against the wall with no where to turn or no way out we find ourselves needing God to reveal Himself to us as being a keeper.

The adversary doesn't have any love for us. Yes, even with our saved, sanctified, Holy Ghost filled self, he doesn't care who your momma or your daddy is! It does not matter what side of the tracks you live on! and it doesn't matter who you know or what your name is! The uncertainty will happen at a time when you least expect it. Even when they do come, it will enable you to recognize that the God we serve is a keeper who kept you in the midst of it all.

Amid sickness and death He kept you; during addiction, failed marriages, toxic relationships, haters hating on you, and in the midst of you doing what you thought you were big and grown enough to do He kept you.

When adversity comes, it does not come with a willingness to fight fair. It has a tendency, to hit you below the belt and where it hurts the most like; having your children acting out! finances being at an all time low! health failing! marriage on the rocks! friends becoming frenemies! folks on the job trying your patience! and let's not forget the church folks who can be a real trip at times because amongst them you're going to find; jealousy, envy, confusion, hurt, backstabbing, lying tongue, and gossip.

The uncertainties of life will throw you a curveball that is looked at as distractions that will steal your joy and peace. With everything you have encountered and been through, with every storm, test, and trial that you had to weather through, and with every tear you had to shed if, you find out that you are still standing in your right mind after the smoke has all cleared then your testimony is one that says, through it all God kept me.

There have been many times in our lives where we can bear witness that with everything we've been through, not only did we experience the keeping power of God, but we knew without question that it was nobody but Him who was able to keep us in all our ways. **(Jude 24) "Now unto Him that is able to keep you from falling and to present you faultless before the presence of his glory with exceeding joy".**

When it says that God is able to keep us from falling it is saying that He is the one who keeps us and not we ourselves. God is capable of doing anything but fail. He is almighty and powerful. With every situation and circumstance that we are confronted with we must understand that it is God who keeps us upright, keeps us from falling literally, and keeps us from sin.

In all his efforts, man does not have the power to keep us in the manner of which we need to be kept no matter how hard he tries nor are we capable of keeping ourselves. Scripture reminds us not only of who it is that is keeping us but also who is with us and for us when being attacked by the adversary. **"For the Lord, your God is he that goeth with you, to fight for you against your enemies." (Deuteronomy 20:4).**

While the enemy is fighting against us, God is always on our side fighting for us. Keeping us, saving us, and protecting us. **"If it had not been for the Lord who was on my side when men rose up against us" (Psalm 124:2).**

To prove the fact that God is always on our side, just ask yourself the question, where would I be if it had not been for the Lord? Well, allow me to tell you. The enemy would have killed you, he would have stolen your joy, peace, and your health. He would have literally destroyed you.

This is what his purpose has been, but by the grace and the mercies of God, we can be grateful that He didn't allow it to be so.

He did not allow the enemy to take us out! God interceded and He keeps interceding on our behalf, keeping us even when it looks like we can't be kept.

Like everyone, I've gone through some rough and hard times. Times when I thought I was going to lose it. Times when I felt like there was no more fight left in me to keep moving forward. But through it all, the Lord himself watched over me. He stood by me as my protector and because He did, I was able to experience the keeping power of a God who is our guardian, our shelter, and our shield.

Man has always tried to take the credit for so many things in life but he cannot take the credit for how blessed I am to look and feel the way I do. All through my life God has cared for provided for and protected me even with my flaws, He loved and kept me through it all. It was His unconditional love for me that never failed me nor did it ever stop. No matter how many times I may have fallen short of His glory He still loved me through all of my mess, inconsistencies, and major downfalls.

It is so good to know that we serve a God who loves us unconditionally. Despite our shortcomings and imperfections, He still loves us. **"But God demonstrates his own love for us in this: While we were still sinners, Christ died for us." (Romans 5:8) NIV.**

When I messed up He kept me; when I stumbled and fell He kept me; when false witnesses rose up against me He kept me; when all hell broke out all around me He kept me and that's why I'm able to profess today that I'm a woman who's kept by God and a well-kept woman I might add.

Often I run into people as I'm sure we all have, who I may not have seen in years. Some of them I have not seen since I graduated from high school and the first thing that is said to me is wow Jackie, you look good! You haven't changed a bit and my response to them is always "HE'S A KEEPER".

All through my life, God has cared for me, provided and protected me, and even with all of my flaws, He loved and kept me through it all.

He's been the keeper of everything that I have and of everyone near and dear to me.

He's kept my home!

He's kept me with a reasonable portion of health and strength!

He's kept me from losing my mind!

He's kept me from things that I never would have thought or dreamed of to happen to me!

To say that God is a keeper is not saying He won't allow some things to happen in our lives, but that as long as we live, there will always be pain, misery, strife, sickness, and death. There will be times when our lives may be affected by some if not all of these situations and we will have to go through it. But if we trust the word of God and stand on His promises we will experience the keeping power of His mighty hand and we will see and know that He is right there with us every step of the way.

Man is always making promises he can't keep. He makes promises to be there with you and for you when the chips are down; he promises to be faithful; he promises to love you always but with every promise that he makes you will hear more of his excuses and lies that will get in the way of him keeping those promises.

Each time he falls short it's because most of the time he only thinks of himself as to what he wants, what he can gain, and what it is you can do for him. But! with God, it's all about us and what He can and will do for us. He wants to bless us; He wants to favor us; He wants us to live an abundant life. A life that's filled with love, joy, peace and happiness. **(John 10:10)** lets us know what satan came to do to us which is to kill, **steal and destroy** but it **also lets us know why Jesus came: "I have come that they might have life and that they might have it more abundantly".**

It 'really' hurts when promises aren't being kept. It can be very disheartening. An unkept promise causes disappointment. When someone makes you a promise you want to believe and trust that they will keep it, but when they don't you lose all hope trust, and faith in anything they say. The truth of the matter is, God is the only one who is worthy of and deserves all of our trust and faith because He always keeps His word. As a child growing up, my grandfather always taught me, my brother, and my cousin that "your word is your bond", meaning do what you say and always keep your promise.

If you are not going to stand by your word and do what you say you are going to do, then don't make the promise to do it. Think before you speak, pick, and choose your words wisely because your word is all you have.

God's word is true, and if we read and study the word, if we apply and live the word, then we will find out that God is a "promise keeper" not a "promise breaker". We will never know of His promises nor will we ever know Him until we are in His word and his word is in us.

It is the word of God that leads us and keeps us. **"Thy word is a lamp unto my feet, and a light unto my path" (Psalm 119:105).** We must have a true and right relationship with God. It is a personal relationship that we should desire to have if we are to know Him for ourselves.

We can never get to know Him if we do not know His word.

God has a purpose and a plan for each one of us, but even though we may not know what those plans and purposes are for our future and what they may hold for us, the blessing is we do know the one who holds our future.

While trying to fulfill those plans and purpose for our lives, we can trust and believe that God is our protector along the way. We can rely on Him to keep us and protect us from the hands of the enemy.

If we are to believe God to be a keeper, we must trust Him in every situation, circumstance, and yes even suffering. We must trust and believe that He will not only keep us amid adversity, but He will keep every promise He has made to us according to His word. **"The Lord is trustworthy in all He promises and faithful in all he does" (Psalm 145:13b) N.I.V.**

He promised: **"I will never leave thee, nor forsake thee" (Hebrews 13:5).** He promised that: **"When thou passest through the waters, I will be with thee; and through the rivers, they shall not overflow; when thou walkest through the fire, thou shall not be burned, neither shall the flame kindle upon thee" (Isaiah 43:2)** He also promised: **"But my God shall supply all your need according to His riches in glory by Christ Jesus" (Philippians 4:19").**

We can never foresee anything happening to us our children any of our family or friends so it behooves us, to always be in prayer. No, we can never be on our knees 24/7 praying, but we can certainly have a praying spirit. Scripture tells us: **"Men ought always to pray, and not faint" (Luke 18:1).**

There is so much going on around us with our families, jobs, health, finances, homelessness, the opioid epidemic, sex trafficking, and particularly with our government that can and will keep us praying 24/7. When walking down the street pray! When you are at work pray! When driving in your car pray! We just need to do as the song by Curt Karr says: I'll pray for you, you pray for me and watch God change things.

We must do what **(Psalm 121:1) says and that is: "I will lift up mine eyes unto the hills, from whence cometh my help. Knowing that my help cometh from the Lord who made heaven and earth."** As well as **(2ⁿᵈ Chronicles 7:14) "If my people, which are called by my name, shall humble themselves and pray, and seek my face, and turn from their wicked ways; then will I hear from heaven, and will forgive their sin, and will heal their land".**

I've experienced many things in life that could have caused me to lose my mind, end up on drugs or alcohol, even being promiscuous but with much prayer and by reading and meditating on His word, God kept me and I just can't thank Him enough. When God shows us how He keeps His promise of how He will bless, keep and protect not only us but our children as well, it can be so overwhelming and it shows us just how much His word is true, full of promise and the security that we have in Him when it says: **"There shall no evil befall thee, neither shall any plague come nigh thy dwelling. For he shall give his angels charge over thee, to keep thee in all thy ways." (Psalm 91:10-11).**

From the time our children are born and as their parents we want so much to protect and keep them from all the traps plots and schemes that the enemy has set up for them. We want so much to safeguard them from hurt, a broken heart, from the betrayal of friends and the attacks of the enemy.

The truth of the matter is, we cannot because there is not but one who can be with our children when we can't! One who can protect them at all times and His name is Jesus.

I truly believe there have been many days in which we found ourselves looking to the hills on behalf of our children knowing where our help comes from. Knowing that God is the only one who can help them and get them through the trials and problems they found themselves facing.

We have got to earnestly pray for our children every day. Asking God to keep them and protect them in their coming and going and during unforeseen dangers.

God has kept us from and even in the midst of so many dangerous situations and by doing so, He has shown us time and time again just how powerful His keeping power is.

It has built up our faith and trust in Him to the point that we don't have any other choice but to have unwavering faith and trust in Him to keep our children.

My #1 Son Carvin, who most people call Cheeks was a victim of an attack in which he found God to be his protector, guardian, and keeper. I was going to attempt to tell his story, but I wasn't there, so I believe it is best if he tells his own story because can't nobody tell your story like you can.

Cheeks Story!

On August 23, 1994, my friends and I were playing basketball at Spruce Street Courts like any other summer night. After we got done playing, we went around the corner to a friend's house on 8th street and just talked and hung out. As it got later and later, one by one each of my friend's made their way home to turn in for the night.

Now the only two people outside on the steps were me and a female friend whom I was dating at the time.

It was now approximately 2 or 3 am, early in the wee hours of the morning on August 24th, which happened to be my 19th birthday.

We sat and talked in the still of the night. You could hear a pin drop, that's how quiet it was. At one point, I happen to look to my left towards Cherry Street and thought I saw a person's head jerk back around the corner as if they were hiding. I didn't pay it too much mind, as it was late and I thought I'm just seeing things.

A few minutes later, a person wearing all black clothing came walking down the street from the area I had just looked at. My friend and I now clearly can see him walking slowly across the street and we had our eyes pierced on him. With our heads turning slowly from left to the center of the street we watched him walk until he disappeared for a split second behind a truck that was parked right across from us. As soon as he passed the truck, he made an about-face and walked in our direction.

I can now see he has a mask and a gun, which was pointed in our direction. We jumped up off the steps and ran towards the door.

When my friend grabbed the doorknob to open the door, it was locked. My heart sunk, as I'm sure hers did. When I turned around my eyes were faced with four guys in all black clothing with masks and guns. Because we were on a porch, our level was slightly above the gunmen.

With guns pointed up in our direction, one of the guys told me to "empty my pockets". I went into my pockets, pulled out a watch, and a beeper, which was all I had from playing ball earlier and I stated "man, I don't have nothing".

One of them came up on the porch and held a gun to my friend while another one came up and hit me in the head with a gun. He didn't hit me that hard to knock me out, but I remember just going down acting as if I were hurt, but I wasn't.

I laid on the ground fearing what was next then he placed a

chromes gun to my head and held it there. After what felt like an eternity, he went through my pockets, kicked me, and then ran off.

I felt relieved that I still had life, but obviously, I was shaken to the core. We were able to knock on the door and my friend's brother who was asleep in the basement opened it.

We explained to him what had just happened and he ran to look outside but of course, saw no one. I went to bed and tried to get some sleep. I can recall being 'really' shaken by the incident and couldn't sleep at all. I remember jumping a few times as anybody would twitching out of fear.

The next day or I should say later on that same day, it was bright and sunny. I will never forget how bright it was. Nothing like a few hours earlier. It was the worst feeling like nobody in this world knew what happened.

Word began to get out and speculation began as to who did what. I can't recall much of what happened after that, but I do remember talking to my mom when she got off work and the both of us being emotional about the situation and being thankful at the same time that I was still here and how God spared my life.

I've been blessed to see and accomplish many things in the last 25 or 26 years on this earth and as my mom would always tell me and trust me, I know it firsthand, that HE'S A KEEPER!!

While my son was telling me what happened, all I could do was thank and praise my God for keeping his powerful hand of protection on him. At the time when all of this was happening to him, he was staying with my mom and all of this took place right around the corner from where she lived. She was sleeping in her bed not knowing what was happening to her grandson and I'm home way across town sleeping in my bed not knowing what was going on with my son. But, the fact of the matter is, we serve a God who when we're sleeping, He's wide awake keeping an eye on our children because of our prayers and

His word that says: **"Behold, he that keepeth Israel shall neither slumber nor sleep" (Psalm 121:4")**.

I truly believe that with all the prayers that I have prayed for and over my son along with his grandparent's prayers, aunties prayers, and the prayer that he prayed that dreadful night is what kept him and has been keeping him all his life.

We've got to keep our children covered in prayer and not only teach them the power of prayer but teach them how and why it's important for them to pray for themselves.

We will never be able to be with our children everywhere they go, but when we know from where our help comes from when we know the one who is always with them we can trust and believe in the word of God that says: **"God is our refuge and strength, A very present help in trouble." (Psalm 46:1)**.

Prayer is the key in every situation and we must always keep our children covered and saturated in prayer. When you know that God is in control of everything concerning you and your children and that He is faithful to His word in never leaving them or forsaking them, then in the words of Pastor Sheryl Brady: "Tell the devil I'm going to bed".

There is no need for us to stay up worrying about anything or trying to fix any situation that is out of our control. God's got it all covered and it's covered by His blood.

I can remember asking him, when the guy knocked you to the ground with your face pressing towards the pavement and a gun to your head, what were you thinking or doing during that time and he said "Mom the only thing I could do" "Pray" and I told him, that God heard your prayer, because a cat could have run past him or somebody could have been walking by and startle him to the point that though he didn't plan on shooting you, he could have pulled that trigger out of nervousness.

Our God is truly a keeper and He proved it that while my son laid on that ground face down at the hands of that gunmen God's mercy said no and He extended His hand of "Divine Protection" and because He did, my son is still here to tell his own story of how God kept him.

If God's eye is watching over the little bitty baby sparrow, then we never ever have to question or wonder if He's watching over us and our children. One thing is for certain, God cares about every one of us and He loves us unconditionally. Not only that, but a baby sparrow is no more valuable than we are to God. (**Fear ye not, therefore, ye are of more value than many sparrows." (Matthew 10:31).**

> If He woke you up this morning – He's a keeper!
> If you have a roof over your head – He's a keeper!
> If you have food on your table – He's a keeper!
> If you have your health and strength – He's a keeper!
> If you've lost a loved one and you're still holding it together it's only because – He's a keeper!

When your momma couldn't keep you! When your daddy forsook you! When your so-called friends turned their backs on you! When your family refused to help you and talked about you, God stepped right in to let you know that He is everything you will ever need and the only one you can count on through all adversity. He's true to His word in that whatever His word says, it will not come back void and you can take it to the bank and invest in it. He's kept all of us through the good times, bad and sad times, lonely and overwhelming times but through it all, our faith got stronger.

No matter what you're going through or facing in life, there is nothing like being kept by the hand, the power, and the blood of Jesus. Just hold on to God's unchanging hand, have faith, and trust in the power of His word and you will definitely experience the keeping power of an awesome God.

PRAYER OF TRUST

Father, in the name of Jesus. Thank you
for being my keeper. You have
kept me so many times and long enough for me to know that I
can trust you with my whole heart, have complete faith
in you, and never doubt your keeping power.
With everything, you kept me through and
from my trust has grown deeper.
I fully know and understand you to be a KEEPER! Amen.

SONG OF ENCOURAGEMENT
"JUST ANOTHER DAY"

Just another day that the Lord has kept me,
Just another day that the Lord has kept me
He kept me from all evil, with my mind stayed on Jesus
Just another day that the Lord has kept me.

By Tessie Hill

3

"The Prayer of Faith"

And the prayer of faith shall save the sick, and the`
Lord shall raise him up; and if he have committed sins,
They shall be forgiven him.

JAMES 5:15

We all have prayed for something or someone at one time or another. We claim to have prayed diligently and that we pray all the time yet God still hasn't answered our prayers.

If God hasn't answered your prayers as of yet, could it be that the words that you speak are empty, they lack power, hope, and expectation? Could it be that the prayer you prayed was nothing but lip service and not sincere coming from your heart?

Maybe you prayed like the Pharisees, praying for yourself and not for others! Or you prayed to make others think that you were more spiritual than they were! So the question I have is this: How are you praying? Are you praying in faith, believing, and trusting that God will do just as you asked Him, or are your prayers full of doubt, doubting that because He hasn't answered you when you wanted Him to or the way you wanted Him to that He won't come through for you? most importantly are you praying for God's will? Asking for His perfect will to be done in your life? Are you asking Him to answer you in His timing and in the way He wants to answer? Or are you continuously praying empty words, doing it in your own strength, trying to fix the problem, work the situation out doing it the way you want? Thinking that if you have a hand in it, it will work out quicker and the way you want it to.

For some people, the reality of their situations is so devastating, that it has them not living up to the expectation of what God can do.

They don't want to risk being disappointed so in praying to God they keep their expectations low. But the fact of the matter is that we serve an awesome and powerful God who is in full control of every problem, trial, and storm that we encounter, so we don't ever have to lower our expectations when it comes to God because He can do all things but fail.

It seems to me that we have put our faith and trust in everything and everyone else but God and they have done nothing but let us down time and time again. The bible reassures us: **"But Jesus beheld them, and said unto them, With men this is impossible; but with God all things are possible." (Matthew 19:26).**

God spoke these words and because He did, we can stand on His word knowing it to be the truth that we can rely and depend on because: **"God is not a man, that he should lie, neither is he the son of man, that he should repent: hath he said, and shall he not do it? Or hath he spoken, and shall he not make it good?" (Numbers 23:19).** God's word will never disappoint us nor will it ever let us down. **"So shall my word be that goeth forth out of my mouth: it shall not return unto me void, but it shall accomplish that which I please, and it shall prosper in the thing whereto I** sent it" (Isaiah 55:11). All we have to do is believe in it because it backs up every move and promise of God.

When we claim Him to be a healer His word says: **"But He was wounded for our transgressions, He was bruised for our iniquities: The chastisement of our peace w as upon Him; And with His stripes, we are healed" (Isaiah 53:5).** When we know Him to be a deliverer, the word says: **"Many are the afflictions of the righteous: but the Lord delivereth him out of them all." (Psalm 34:19).** If you are mourning and grieving because of the loss of a loved one His promise says: **"Blessed are they that mourn, for they shall be comforted" (Matthew 5:4)** and **"Weeping may endure for a night, but joy cometh in the morning" (Psalm 30:5).** When life overwhelms you and when man fails you, you've got to embrace the word of God have faith in the word and pray the prayer of faith.

When we pray the prayer of faith, we are praying with the expectancy of God hearing, understanding, caring and answering our prayers in a way that will not only blow our minds but the devil's mind as well. We'll pray with the confidence and belief that He will show up and show out for us right in the nick of time every time. In the words of Dottie Peoples, "He may not come when you want Him, but He'll be there right on time. He's an on-time God, oh yes He is!

As Christians, prayer for us ought to be a lifestyle and not as a needed attempt to pray only when we want something from God or needing Him to do something for us.

I'm sure we've all heard it being said that we should pray and thank God in the good times as well as the bad times. When things are working out for us and even when they aren't. The consolation we have in those words is: **"And we know that all things work together for good to them that love God, to them who are the called according to his purpose" (Romans 8:28).** No matter how bad things may seem to get in our lives, as long as we love God and draw closer to

Him through His Word, we can have faith in His wonderful promise believing that He will always work our situations out for our good.

It is so imperative that we always pray because prayer is the key to every problem. It is a powerful spiritual weapon, that we have to fight against the enemy. It is desperately needed in our lives when seeking healing for the sick, deliverance for those who are in bondage, and to comfort those who are grieving and broken-hearted. Most importantly, prayer is the component that keeps us connected to the true power source of Jesus Christ.

Prayer through faith can move mountains. It says so in the word of God: "**Jesus answered and said unto them, Verily I say unto you, if ye have faith, and doubt not, ye shall not only do this which is done to the fig tree, but also if ye shall say unto the mountain, be thou removed, And be thou cast into the sea; it shall be done. And all things, whatsoever ye shall ask in prayer, believing, ye shall receive**" (Matthew 21:21-22).

When praying, we cannot pray as the Pharisees prayed, praying for show, praying to make others think that we're more spiritual than they are, or praying more for ourselves than we are for others. None of these things are impressive to God. He knows the sincerity of our hearts and He also knows the motives behind what and how we pray.

We serve an all-knowing God who knows if and when we are putting our complete faith and trust in Him when we pray. We may be able to fool men by professing how much we know God and His Word, but we can never fool God. We need to stop being so hypocritical saying one thing and doing another. With God, it is not so much about what we say but more about our actions. So no matter how many times you try to hide behind a mask when coming to the throne of grace seeking answers, help, or direction from God, He always sees behind your mask and sees into your thoughts and motives. There is nothing that can be kept or hidden from God. **"They say they know God, but their actions speak louder than their words. They're real creeps, disobedient good-for-nothings" (Titus 1:16) MSG**

In **(1ˢᵗ Thessalonians 5:17)** we are instructed to **"Pray without ceasing",** meaning pray continuously, nonstop! There are times when we don't even feel like praying, or know how to pray but we must pray anyway. Pray through our hurt and pain! Pray through our frustrations and disappointments. Pray when you find yourself entering into a storm, during a storm, and coming out of a storm. Pray! Pray! Pray!

Prayer is that spiritual weapon that we should use before we start murmuring and complaining. When we go through life murmuring and complaining we get nothing accomplished and we definitely cannot be pleasing unto God. It shows a sign of disbelief and doubt in the proficiency of what God can do. But when we pray and pray in faith God will do just what His word says He will do . **"And whatsoever ye shall ask in my name, that will I do, that the Father may be glorified in the Son." If ye shall ask anything in my name, I will do it"** (John 14: 13-14).

If we're not careful, we could very easily fall into the habit of not praying at all and it is so easy to do. We should never look at prayer as being our last resort rather we should look at it as being our first option.

> "We tend to use prayer as a last resort, but
> God wants it to be our first line of defense.
> We pray when there's nothing else we can do,
> but God wants us to pray before we do anything at all."
> Oswald Chambers

There is always something or someone that requires us to pray, and even though it's not possible for us to be on our knees praying continuously or nonstop, we should have a praying spirit whereby we can pray for the sick, the homeless, the underprivileged, grieving families, drug and alcohol addiction and human sex trafficking all while we are driving in our cars, walking down the street, in the market, and on our jobs.

We all need to have a praying spirit that prays no matter where we are, who we're around, or what we're doing.

Prayer is essential in each of our lives and so we must pray, believe and trust, that God will hear our cry and answer our prayers according to what His perfect will is for us, being mindful that our will must line up with God's will and that we must pray continually.

God's will most times calls for us to be patient and wait on Him to make a move in our situation, but waiting seems to be a hard and difficult thing for us to do but the word of God tells us: **"But they that wait upon the Lord shall renew their strength; They shall mount up with wings eagles; They shall run, and not be weary, And they shall walk, and not faint"** (Isaiah 40:31). It also tells us: **"And let us not be weary in well-doing; for in due season we shall reap If we faint not"** (Galatians 6:9).

If we just learn to wait patiently and stop trying to have everything microwave-ready, God will renew our strength, He will give us the strength we need to hold on to His unchanging hand, and He will give us the strength we need to endure until the end. It is time to soar above our problems and if we don't get weary and faint not God will take us into our due season. When will we learn that we cannot hurry God, He doesn't move according to our timetable or agenda but only His.

God knows what's best for us and sees what we cannot see. He sees the traps He hears the plots and schemes that are being set up for us. He knows who is for us and who is against us. We can only see what is in front of us but God can see what is down the road ahead of us on each side of us and in the back of us all at the same time. That is more than enough reason why we should wait on Him and trust Him.

I have heard it said time and time again that I'm waiting on God to move or waiting to hear from God, when in fact He could be waiting on us. Waiting on us to pray earnestly and to have faith in Him completely. Waiting on us to lean on Him depend on Him and in the words of one of our church members the Late Evelyn Bailey there will be times you'll have to lay on Him. God is always faithful to His promises and He will deliver whether it is now or later.

Nothing about life is for certain and it is sure to disappoint us and let us down, but when we pray the will of the Father by faith and allow our will to line up with His we will get through whatever we're going through as long as we wait on Him.

Praying the prayer of faith requires us to have faith to see beyond what we do see, and to have faith you've got to know the word of God.

It is the word of God that produces our faith. It is the written word of God coming alive in our hearts and becoming real to us. "So then faith cometh by hearing and hearing by the word of God" (Romans 10:17).

You cannot have faith in a God you know nothing about. If you do not know what He is able to do His word tells us: "Now unto Him, that is able to do exceeding abundantly above all that we ask or think, according to the power that worketh in us" (Ephesians 3:20) His word tells us: "He that loveth not knoweth not God; for God is love" (1st John 4:8). If you do not know what His promises are it tells us in His word: "For all promises of God In him are yea and in him Amen, unto the glory of God by us" (1st Corinthians 1:20).

God is a prayer-answering God and I know that to be a fact. I can't count how many times He's answered my prayers as they are too numerous to tell. I can only say that I wasn't always doing and saying the right thing but when I prayed to Him even in my messed up state I'm so grateful that He heard my cry, looked beyond every one of my faults, saw my needs, answered my prayers and brought me out to the other side of through. I believe He answered my prayers because He knew my heart and He saw that I was praying with the right motives.

We must understand, that we can't pray to God harboring bitterness, anger, jealousy, and unforgiveness in our hearts, expecting an answer from God. He is not looking at our outer appearance when we pray. Anything that we have in our hearts that is not of God He sees, for truly He is an examiner of the heart. **"But the Lord said to Samuel, Do not look on his appearance or on the height of his stature, because I have rejected him. For the Lord sees not as man sees: man looks on the outward appearance, but the Lord looks on the heart" (1ˢᵗ Samuel 16:7). ESV**

When we pray we don't have to go through anyone to get an answer and we don't need anyone to go for us. The word of God gives us an invitation and the free will to come before Him: **"Let us, therefore, come boldly unto the throne of grace, that we may obtain mercy, and find grace to help in time of need" (Hebrews 4:16).**

This invitation lets us know that we don't have to be timid, weak, or uncomfortable when we go before God in prayer. It says "come boldly" not "arrogantly". We may have been given the invitation to come before Him boldly, but it doesn't' mean haughty, proud, or full of yourself. It means to come with the confidence and assuredness of believing and trusting in God and His word. **"Pride cometh before destruction, And an haughty spirit before a fall" (Proverbs 16:11).**

Every time we come before the Lord in prayer we've got to humble ourselves. **"Humble yourselves in the sight of the Lord, and He shall lift you up" (James 4:10).** With a humble spirit, God is ready and willing to lift you up out of any situation or problem you may find yourself in, any hardship that may befall you, and any financial strain you may have but we first must humble ourselves.

We all stand in need of God to make some things happen and to change some things for us in our lives. We need Him to deliver our sons and daughters, save our spouses, open up some doors that are for us and close the ones that are not. We need Him to heal our bodies, and with everything we need for Him to do, there are some things He needs for us to do, and have humility is one of them. Actually, it is a requirement: **"If my people which are called by name, shall humble themselves and pray, and seek my face, and turn from their wicked ways; then will I hear from heaven, and will forgive their sin, and will heal their land" (2ⁿᵈ Chronicles 7:14).**

I've already stated before, that while we're waiting on God to do something He's waiting on us to do something which is found here in this passage of scripture of (2ND Corinthians 7:14). God is telling us that we must first humble ourselves, pray, seek His face, and turn from our wicked ways, then He will hear our prayer, forgive us of our sin, and heal the land. We just have to do what we are instructed to do. We are to be obedient to the word of God and when we are, He will allow His perfect will to be done.

There will come a time when everyone will be faced with a situation that will come as a total surprise and they will find that it is totally out of their control. It will be so overwhelming and devastating that they will lose faith, hope, and start doubting and questioning God. But when we hold on to our faith and hope and let go of doubt, cease from questioning God and stand on that portion of scripture that says: **"calleth those things which be not as though they were"(Romans 4:17),** they will find themselves praying a sincere prayer that's from the heart, not wavering in their faith and not having an ulterior motive for what you are praying to God for, He will come through for you every time.

Aunt Gearls Story

It all began in 1965 when my aunt Gearl got married to her hus-band James Harley. They got married at my grandparent's home on October 30, 1965. I had only been playing the piano for a short period when she had asked me to play the Bridal March for her as she came down the steps. Boy was I excited and nervous all at the same time.

The wedding was small and intimate. It was mostly our family in attendance. My grandmother's sister aunt Roberta and her husband uncle Junious along with a few of our cousins from Baltimore came to the wedding.

We had a great and memorable time. She was dressed in blue, which was her favorite color and my Mom stood with her in her fa-vorite color pink. We all were so happy for them both. Joy was truly in the air.

For their honeymoon, they drove to Canada and stayed for a week.

I was really close to my aunt. She was like a second mother to me and I was that daughter that she never had. I could talk to her about any and everything that was going on with me. I just couldn't wait until she got back.

Upon their return, life as it was when they left was not the same as when they returned. Our whole family's life was turned upside down.

One thing about our family is that at that time we were a small closely knit family, the only difference today is that we are still closely knit just not as small.

We are the kind of family that when one of us go through we all go through; when one of us hurts we all hurt; when one of us lacks, we all pull together and help by any means necessary.

When they returned home, Gearl got sick. We took her to the hospital to have her checked out but after checking her out, we were told that they would like to keep her to run more tests. So they ran a test for a couple of days and the result was that she had Lupus.

The doctor came to us and said that she was very sick and that she had a chronic case of Lupus. She continued to remain in the hospital for about another week during which time James her husband took sick and he was admitted into the hospital as well. Talk about being overwhelmed. This whole situation was unbelievable and overwhelming, but I was convinced that because of my Christian background and the teachings of my Grandparents, Mother, and Aunt that even at the age of fourteen I knew who to turn to in times of distress and His name is Jesus. **"When my heart is overwhelmed lead me to the rock that is higher than I" (Psalm 61:2).**

I knew what the power of prayer could and would do. I was blessed to have grown up in a family who prayed, knew how to pray, and got results when they prayed.

My family had been praying for my aunt as well as my uncle but it seemed as though nothing was changing for the better. Gearl was getting worse.

One day while visiting with her the doctor came into her room to tell us that she wasn't getting any better, that he had done everything possible for her, that it's only a matter of time, and that he would give her a week or two at the most.

These were the words that my family and I were faced with regarding her present situation and condition.

My Aunt who was only 35 years old, just got married and looking to live a happy and prosperous life with her new husband is now laying in the hospital bed with a chronic case of Lupus having only a week or two at most to live according to the report of the doctor.

When the doctor gave us that report I can remember my eyes filling up with water, tears falling from my eyes in disbelief about what he just told us. At the same time, while standing around Gearls bedside,

I began looking at my Mom, Christine Bailey, and my Grandparents Deacon and Deaconess Louis and Mollie Graham who outwardly didn't seem to be moved nor did they show any signs of being worried by what the doctor's report was.

I saw such strength and belief in the power of prayer that I know it is the reason why I have that same faith and belief in the power of prayer and what it can do today.

It is because of them that I believe by faith that whatever I'm praying for or whomever I'm praying for God will answer my prayer.

My granddaughter Ariyon, who is eighteen, shared with me an assignment she had to do for school, which was a presentation about her family and how she came from good strong stock. Well, I too share that same sentiment of coming from a good strong stock of prayer warriors.

It was during this time of my aunt's diagnosis, that I experienced the true working power of prayer and what it can do. I was able to not only see but to be a part of a prayer vigil alongside my grandparents and mother held around her bedside. At the age of fourteen is when I truly began developing a prayer life.

When I saw such strength in my family, it lets me know today that when the question is being asked whose report do you believe? my response will always be, I shall believe the report of the Lord and His report says that by His stripes I am healed.

What I saw was them showing without saying a word their strength and belief that says we serve a God who when you say you can't He says He will.

This is what they were believing for my aunt that by His stripes she is healed. Because they only gave Gearl a week or two to live, they allowed James to be put in the same room with her. In their minds, I guess they were saying she doesn't have long so let him be with her for as long as he can.

To have him put into the same room was something I had never heard of before, but God has a way of doing what He does so that it will leave us without any doubt and no question that it was all God who not only healed Gearl but James as well.

We heard loud and clear when the doctor said they did all they could do and couldn't do anything more to help heal Gearl, but we also knew that there is still one who was capable and able to hold back the night and heal her if it was His perfect will. All we had to do was ask and believe by faith that all would be well. **"And this is the confidence that we have in Him, that, if we ask anything according to his will, he heareth us: And if we know that he hear us, whatsoever we ask, we know that we have the petitions that we desired of Him (1ˢᵗ John 5:14-15).**

It was decided by my Grandparents that we would hold a prayer vigil in that room every day until the Lord's will is done. How inspiring it was for me, a fourteen-year-old to see the authority that my Grandparents took over this illness that was trying to take the life of their daughter, my Mom's sister, and my Aunt. It just was not going to happen under our watch.

Every day we prayed. We took turns praying. Their room was never left without one, two, or all of us being in there praying. The presence and the power of God was truly felt in that room. *"Where two or three are gathered together in my name, there am I in the midst of them" (Matthew 18:20).*

We continued to pray on one accord because we needed healing and we believed that God was the only one who could do anything about our need. We weren't praying out of desperation but rather, we were praying by faith for a desperate situation.

We went to Him boldly, unwavering in our faith and trust in Him that He would hear our cry, see our hearts, and know that the only intent we had in coming before His throne was to seek His face, asking for a healing touch for Gearl and James. **"Then shall ye call upon me, and ye shall go and pray unto me, and I will hearken unto you" (Jeremiah 29:12).**

During the prayer vigil, we knew that God was hearing our cry because James was getting better and within a few days, he was finally released from the hospital. Gearl however, was not getting any better but we were thanking God that she was not getting worst and so we kept praying. Yes, we kept praying, because of the faith that we had in believing that just because Gearl had not gotten any better didn't negate the fact that **"Jesus is the same yesterday, today and forever" (Hebrew 13:8)** and that if He did it for James surely He was going to do it for Gearl. We stood on the word of God that says: **"Now faith is the substance of things hoped for, the evidence of things not seen" (Hebrews 11:1).**

To have that type of faith is to say that you have to see it before you see it. We had to see Gearl healed before she was healed. We had to **"call those things that be not as though they were" (Romans 4:17).** We had to call forth her healing before we even saw it in Jesus name.

Prayer is the one thing we cannot live without. We cannot make it through life without it. Prayer keeps us when we need to be kept; it covers us when we need to be covered, and it provides for us when we need provision.

Prayer is the one thing that is needed for our survival as well as to keep us connected to God, just like an umbilical cord is needed to keep a baby connected to its mother for survival while in the womb.

It was going into the second week of the continued prayer vigil, that Gearl was beginning to show some signs of getting better. We couldn't help but to thank and praise God for what He had already done.

She made it through one of the two weeks that the doctor gave her. No, she was not completely healed of Lupus but the blessing is that the Lord saw fit to allow her to make it through the first week and that was a sign to us that God was at work. Week two came and went and she was still here and was able to live with the symptoms of it for years to come. At the end of the second week, she was well enough to go home and we couldn't have been any more grateful because you see, God had held back the night and the doctor's report was null and void.

I am a firm believer in doctors and I know that they are a blessing from the Lord, but I also know that all power does not lie in their hands only in the hands of God.

They have gone to school to learn many things about the anatomy of the body, but God is the creator of the body and no one knows the body better than the creator Himself, God.

I would never tell anyone not to go to the doctors nor would I ever tell anyone not to take medicine prescribed to you. Go to the doctors, take the medicine but also take whatever report you get from them to the Lord in prayer and trust God, believe God, and have faith in God for your healing. Know that He is Jehovah Rapha, He is the Balm in Gilead, He is a Healer and He is the true Physician.

We never heard Gearl complain. She took her medicine as directed and did what she was supposed to do. After some years had passed, we could see the toll Lupus was taking on her body. She had crippling Rheumatoid Arthritis, aching joints, stiffness, swelling, and at times extreme fatigue but she persevered and lived with those symptoms for a long time and she never complained.

My Aunt Gearl was a prayer warrior in her own right. She knew the power of prayer and she knew what prayer had done for her when she was diagnosed with Lupus. She was a firm believer in knowing what the power of prayer would do and could do in any situation.

Whenever anyone came to her with a problem, her response

would always be "let's pray about it". She enjoyed praying for people so much so that she had a prayer ministry over the phone.

The saints from the church would call her for prayer and when she was finished praying, the folks would feel better and situations were turned around.

In growing up in a family who knew the true worth of prayer and the power of it, I can say for myself that I too know the power of prayer. I too know what the power of prayer can do and will do because I saw with my own eyes how praying without ceasing, praying, trusting and believing, praying with power, and praying with unwavering faith will allow you to witness the true working power of our Lord and Savior Jesus Christ. It will reveal to you what God is able to do. **"Now unto Him, that is able to do exceeding abundantly above all that we ask or think, according to the power that worketh in us" (Ephesians 3:20).**

The doctor's report said that she only had about a week or two to live, but the report of the Lord said differently. God showed those doctors who was in control of this situation. God in His grace and mercy did not give my aunt one week or two weeks, one year or two years. He added 40 more years to her life. She was diagnosed at the young age of 35 and lived to be 75 at which time the Lord took her home. Won't He do it? I am a firm believer that those 40 years added to her life was the result of her parents, sister, and niece taking authority over her illness by holding a prayer vigil and Praying the Prayer of FAITH.

PRAYER OF FAITH...

Father God in the name of Jesus I come to you understanding
and knowing the power of prayer. Thank you for the
many prayers You answered even when it seemed as though
I couldn't pray for myself. I know now that all I have to do
is pray without ceasing and know the importance of
Praying in faith. Amen.

SONG OF ENCOURAGEMENT
"I KNOW WHAT PRAYER CAN DO"

I know what prayer can do
I know what prayer can do
I know what prayer can do
I know what prayer can do
I found the answer in prayer
I'll tell it everywhere, I know, I know, I know, what prayer can do

I know He'll see you through
I know He'll see you through
I know He'll see you through
I know He'll see you through
I found the answer in prayer
I'll tell it everywhere cause I Know, I know, I know what prayer can do

Prayer can heal the sick
Prayer can raise the dead
I remember one day five thousand souls were fed

I found the answer in prayer
I'll tell it everywhere I know, I know, I know what prayer can do

I know that prayer, prayer changes things
I know that prayer, prayer changes things
I've been out on the stormy sea
Out on the stormy sea, stormy raging sea

I've been hungry
I've been sick
I've been filled with misery
But Jesus came, Jesus came along and He rescued me
I found the answer and I will tell it everywhere, cause I know, I know
I know what prayer can do.

By: Jesse Dixon

4

"Out of the Box"

"And Peter answered him and said, Lord, if it be thou, bid me come unto thee on the water, And he said, Come, And when Peter was come down out of the ship, he walked on the water, to go to Jesus."

MATTHEW 14:28-29

So many of us live a life that keeps us in bondage. A life that keeps us feeling fearful. It keeps us wrapped up, tangled up, and tied up all because we are afraid to make a move or dare to do something different that is out of the norm. Fearful of what people might think or say about us when we do something that they are not used to seeing us do. But in the word of God it tells us **"For God hath not given us the spirit of fear, but of power, and of love, and of a sound mind" (2nd Timothy 1:7).** It also lets us know that: **The Lord is my light and my salvation; whom shall I fear? The Lord is the strength of my life; of whom shall I be afraid? (Psalm 27:1).** In other words, there is nothing or no one we need to fear. With God on our side, we don't have to fear anything or anyone.

Fear is not of God rather faith is. When we have fear, what it is saying is that God I don't believe that you can or that you are able; It says that we believe more in what the adversary is saying more than what God is saying.

The adversary says "you are a failure" but the word of God says **"For a just man falleth seven times, and riseth up again: But the wicked shall fall into mischief" (Proverbs 24:16).**

When the adversary says "you can't" God's word says: **"I can do all things through Christ which strengtheneth me" (Philippians 4:13).** When the adversary says "nobody wants to be bothered with you and you're made to feel rejected", the word of God reminds us: **"He came unto his own, and his own received him not. But as many as received him, to them gave He the power to become the sons of God, even to them that believe on his name" (John 1:11-12).**

We do not ever have to be worried or concerned about what satan the adversary has to say about us because he will do and say whatever he deems necessary to get and to keep us in disobedience towards God. He will do and say whatever it takes to draw and pull us away from whatever it is God has set our hands to do that will be beneficial for the upbuilding of the Kingdom of God and His glory.

We've got to understand that the enemy doesn't' want to see us blessed. He does not want to see us succeed or be prosperous and so he keeps having us to look back instead of looking and reaching forward.

He figures if he can keep us in a box, doubting and questioning ourselves, caring and worried about what other people say, then he does not have to concern himself about us coming out the box being who God says we are which is: **"I am a child of God", "But as many as received him, to them gave he power to become the sons of**

God, even to them that believe on His name" (John 1:12). He says "I am chosen": "According to him as he hath chosen us in him before the foundation of the world, that we should be holy and without blame before him in love" (Ephesians 1:4). "I am God's workmanship", "For we are his workmanship, created in Christ Jesus unto good works, which God hath before ordained that we should walk in them." (Ephesians 2:10). "I am redeemed" "In whom we have redemption through his blood, the forgiveness of sins, according to the riches of his grace" (Ephesians 1:7). "I am a new creature in Christ" "Therefore if any man be in Christ, he is a new creature: old things are passed away; behold, all things have become new" (2nd Corinthians 5:17).

The adversary looks at us and wants to treat us like that toy that has been around for decades. It is called the Jack-in-the-Box. Most of us had one, I know I did.

This toy had a clown who was called Jack inside a box, which had a crank on the side that had to be turned until Jack popped out of the box.

The key to this toy was that you never knew when he was going to pop out and that would be the surprise. You would keep turning while the music kept playing, and when the music stopped playing, Jack would pop out of the box. Once he popped out you would push him back in the box, turn the crank and wait for him to pop out again.

It was so much fun seeing Jack pop out of that box, waiting in such anticipation for his surprise exit, but it was much more fun trying to put him back in because there were times when he gave a little resilience by being a little springy while trying to push him back in that box. When pushing him back in the box you would have to be quick to close the top so he would stay in the box until the next time you turned the crank.

It's pretty much how satan gets enjoyment out of turning the crank in our lives, that when we come out of our comfort zones, he's right there ready to put us back in a box, thinking that he's in control and when we try to come out of the box he keeps trying to push us back in by coming at us with fear, anxiety, low self-esteem, and doubt. But the God we serve who draws near to us as we draw near to Him will not allow satan to put us back in a box that He brought us out of.

If we find ourselves back in the box once God brought us out then we have only ourselves to blame and most times when we go back it's because that's where we feel more comfortable and it's what we're used to.

It is a feeling like what the Israelites felt when God instructed Moses to lead them out of Egypt. Here it is, Moses is leading them out of bondage and they complained and murmured that they had no meat to eat.

They referred back to Egypt (in the box) where they were held in bondage and complained about how well they ate: **"The Israelites said, "Why didn't God let us die in comfort in Egypt where we had lamb stew and all the bread we could eat? You've brought us out into this wilderness to starve us to death, the whole company of Israel!" (Numbers 16:3) MSG**

It is not God's intention for us to stay in a box! He does not want us to be stuck in a place that will keep us from doing all that He has designed for us to do. He doesn't want us to go back to Egypt once He has brought us out.

It is okay to look back, but you must not go back. Look back over your life as to how He brought you through! Look back as to where He brought you from! Look back as to how He kept you in the midst of it all.

When you look back and see how He brought you through then it will give you the hope and strength you need to make it through even now.

Boxes were made to keep the contents of what's in it contained. They are to keep what is in it from coming out and we must understand that God is in the business of delivering us and not containing us. He is in the business of bringing us out of the darkness into the marvelous light and not keeping us hidden in the dark hiding us from the light.

If when we find ourselves feeling confined, restricted, repressed, and suppressed that's the time when we should seek God even the more asking Him to deliver us and lose the shackles that have us bound. satan gets great pleasure out of keeping us pumped up with fear, keeping us stagnant making us paralyzed with fear so that we will be afraid to make a move towards the things of God. He likes it because it makes him feel like he is large and in charge and in complete control of our lives. But what he doesn't understand is that God was, is, and always will be in full control of our lives. satan does not have unlimited power, he is limited to do anything against God's people even limited to taking our life. **"And the Lord said unto satan, behold, he is in thine hand, but save his life"** **(Job 2:6).** he cannot be everywhere at once and he doesn't know everything concerning us. he does not know our thoughts, he does not know what the future holds for us, and he certainly does not know our hearts.

Our God is an originator and satan will always be a duplicator. There is none like our God. He is in a class all by himself. There is none before Him and there will be none after Him. He is always and forever the great I am that I am, He is always and forever the beginning and ending through all eternity. **"I am Alpha and Omega, the beginning and the ending, saith the Lord, which is, and which was and which is to come, the Almighty" (Revelation 1:8).** God always was and always will be.

Everything that satan does or tries to do to us has to have God's permission to do it. he may make moves to destroy us, to cause us to lose faith, to doubt and question God, and even to distract us from our focus and the plans God has for us, but he is still a loser. After all these years, decades, and centuries that he has been defeated, he should know by now that our God always has the last and final say and move. We can be encouraged in the word of God that says: **"For I know, the plans I have for you, declares the Lord, plans to prosper you and not to harm you, plans to give you hope and a future." (Jeremiah 29:11) N.I.V.**

God knows everything concerning us. He knows the plans, He knows when, where, and how His plans are going to work out for us.

Whatever God has set for us to do in life, we don't have to allow satan to fill us up with fear or keep us bound and limited in a box.

Even when fear creeps up through the cracks of our lives we can do whatever God's plan is for our lives because we know who is for us and who is with us. Even if fear rises up to prevent you from doing and being all that God has planned for you, do it anyway, even if you have to do it afraid.

When I think back over my life, I can remember a time when I came out of the box. I was afraid because it was something new and different for me but because I knew and trusted the one who was turning the crank on that box that released me, I popped out and did what He told me to do anyway and I did it afraid.

The Unforseen Journey!

In 1980, I had left my home church along with about fifty other members due to a split that hurt me to my core and I vowed I was not going to go to another church or have any more dealings with church folks. I was done with it all, but it became very apparent to me that God was not done with me.

While at my home church I was very much involved in different ministries. I sang with the Voices of Faith Choir, President of the BYF (Baptist Youth Fellowship), assisted my grandmother in teaching 3rd grade Sunday school, and played the piano for the Youth Choir. Mr., Ted Brooks whom I admired, was the Minister of music and he had begun teaching me to play the organ.

When the split came about he found out how I was feeling about not attending another church and when he did, he sat me down and talked to me. He told me that he did not want me to sit on my gift of playing the piano and he suggested that I go visit a church that he knew needed someone to play for their choir.

I can remember giving him a rough time, but I gave in and told him I would go visit.

I asked him what was the name of the church, and he said Mt. Olive C.M.E Church. I looked at him and said, "that's a Methodist Church" he said yes and "the same God that's here in the Baptist Church is the same God that is in the Methodist Church." All I ever knew was Baptist and I was second-guessing going to a Methodist Church, but because I gave Mr. Ted my word, I went.

One thing I will always remember my Grandfather teaching me my brother and cousin is that your word is your bond, and if folks cannot depend on your word, they will never be able to depend on you.

Everyone except for Charles (Bus) Gadden and myself went to St. John Baptist Church. Personally, I did not feel I was ready to be a part of another congregation. I was not fully over the hurt I was feeling of leaving the church I was born and raised in.

It was in December that I decided I would go visit Mt. Olive. Upon my arrival, I sat in the back on the last pew close to the door so as not to disturb anyone if I decided to exit. After being there a while, I noticed they only had about five people in the choir with no musician and as I looked around there were only about ten to twelve members sitting in the pews.

I thought to myself, this is a small congregation but the strange thing was, I felt quite comfortable sitting there. Next thing I knew, a lady by the name of Mrs. Alethia Prater did the announcements and welcomed the visitors. I remembered Mrs. Prater as a kid growing up not knowing this is where she attended. She kept looking at me as if she knew who I was but wasn't quite sure if it was me. She then yelled out Jackie is that you? I replied, yes it's me Mrs. Prater and she proceeded to welcome me. She knew I played the piano and now I'm praying that she would not ask me to come play and she didn't. Before I knew it, a young man came out to the pulpit who just happened to be the Pastor and his name was Rev. Ronald Davis.

This man of God preached like I had never heard the word preached before. I was so intrigued by him and I guess it was because, God allowed me to see that a preacher called by Him will do just what he was called to do which is to preach the gospel whether he's Methodist, Baptist, or Pentecostal and Rev. Davis preached and I was truly blessed by the word.

Yes, I found out that the services were different, but just as Mr. Ted told me "the same God that's in the Baptist church is the same God in the Methodist Church." My spirit was so uplifted and I did not feel that weight of hurt, disappointment, and anger I felt when I first came in. I was so uplifted that I came back the next Sunday and then the next Sunday until I joined. I was being so blessed by the word and I developed such a love for the people that I thought I would never have since leaving my home church.

When it comes to the things of God, we can never say never. I thought I would never go to another church, but I did, I thought I would never allow myself to be close with the folks of the church, but I did. I even ended up playing for the choir, which I enjoyed.

I was feeling hopeful again. Every part of me was feeling rejuvenated up until the Sunday that came when we were told that Rev. & Mrs. Davis would be leaving us going to another church. When I heard that news, I was devastated. I just could not believe that God would bring me here to build me up and have me feel so shattered by this news.

Rev. Davis had been at Mt. Olive for the past three or four years and never in my wildest imagination did I think he would be leaving us.

This was the one thing I did not like nor could I get used to in the Methodist church. It would be nothing for them to decide at the Annual Conference who would be coming back and who would be leaving.

I remained at Mt. Olive for six years and during that time, we had at least four different Pastors.

It was not until the fifth Pastor came that the Lord spoke to my heart to let me know that it was time for me to move on. Even though I knew what my main purpose was which was to serve the Lord it was really difficult for me to adjust to the leadership of the different Pastor's that were assigned to us.

I had been wrestling with the fact of leaving Mt. Olive mainly because I would be leaving them without a pianist, but the Lord worked it all out for my good.

While He was working it all out for me, I had to trust Him through it all. I had to do what the word of God instructs us to do: **"Trust in the Lord with all thine heart, and lean not unto thine own understanding. In all thy ways acknowledge Him, and He shall direct thy paths" (Pro verbs 3:5&6).**

The Lord instructed me to write a letter of resignation at which time our new Pastor Rev. Jones was assigned to us. I remember telling God with such a heavy heart, that I could not write the letter and that He would have to be the one to write that letter for me.

I had established such a wonderful and great love and relationship with the members that I could not begin to find the words to say I'm leaving. The thought of leaving them was so heavy on my heart, but God showed Himself faithful. He spoke the words to my heart and I was able to write the letter.

The first Sunday Rev. Jones came to us he asked to have a meeting directly after service. When we gathered together for the meeting I sat next to Mrs. Prater and the whole time I was a nervous wreck about having to read my letter, but the Lord interceded on my behalf by having Mrs. Prater say to me "you're leaving us aren't you??

When she said that to me I got so filled up to the point of having tears in my eyes. I never said anything to her or anyone for that matter regarding my leaving but because she asked I knew that only God could have revealed that to her.

I answered yes, but I was struggling. She then said to me "if the Lord is directing you to leave then you have to do what He tells you". She then proceeded to ask if what I was holding in my hand was my resignation letter, and I said yes and she asked me if I wanted her to read it and by now you must know what my answer was.

After she read the letter, Rev. Jones could see how hard this was for me and he kind of made light of it by saying "I hope your decision to leave doesn't have anything to do with my coming here" we all laughed but I assured him that it had nothing to do with him personally.

My reason for leaving was due to the fact, that, I did not feel I was being fed like when I first started. I felt like my light was going out. I could not let my true feelings be made known but God knew.

I did tell the Pastor which was the truth that I was being led by God to leave.

Rev. Jones let me know how sorry he was about my leaving, but he asked if I could do him a favor? I replied to him yes if I could.

The favor he asked of me was to hold off for a couple of months before leaving because he was hopeful that his wife who suffered back injury during an accident they had coming from the Annual Conference would be able to attend service and play for the choir and the service. I replied very enthusiastically with yes I could stay.

Through this whole ordeal, the Lord worked every detail out for me down to even the First Lady being a Pianist. Every concern I had about leaving, God had already worked it out.

The six years I spent at Mt. Olive, I look at as a time God had set aside for my healing from the split. I call Mt. Olive my healing station.

He knew I was not ready to move on to a large congregation and so He sent me to this small congregation in number but big on love and compassion.

It was a time that God had to do a work in me to prepare me for what He had in store for me.

My husband at that time belonged to Friendship Baptist Church. They too needed a musician so I attended service and played for both the youth and Senior Choir.

I so enjoyed attending the services and had a great relationship with the Pastor the late Rev. Sydney Mills, but I still did not feel as if this is where I was supposed to be.

The first Sunday in October 1988, was my first time attending a service at St. John Baptist Church and at that service, I was moved by the Holy Spirit to join. Finally, I felt like I was at home. I enjoyed everything about the service especially the word being preached by such an anointed man of God.

Once I became a member, I joined The Townsend Ensemble which was a choir named after our Pastor Rev. Dr. Silas M. Townsend. Joining the Townsends was something that I needed and was blessed to be a part of.

When I joined, Minister J. Teddy Johnson who is an anointed psalmist and organist played for us and Barry Pittman was our Director. After being a member for about a year, I was voted in as president which was a shock to me because I was only a member for a year and I didn't think I was known well enough by the members to be their president, but it was quite evident to me, that this was a move of God and it was what He had planned for me.

It was not long after I became a member and President of the Townsend's, that Teddy and his family moved to Las Vegas and we were without an organist, but the Lord blessed and gave us a young man who was anointed to play by the name of Solomon Cummings.

Solomon was one of the fifty members who left my home church and came to St. John. He was brought to my home church by the new pastor who was the cause for the split. Solomon played for The Voices of Faith Choir of which I was a member and we acquired a great relationship with him.

The plan for bringing Solomon there was with the intention of making him the organist of the youth choir that I was playing for. That was the Pastor's plan but it certainly was not the plan of God.

When we left, Solomon said, "if ya'll leave, I'm leaving to." When we trust God to work out our problems we can be assured that He will work out every detail for our good. **"But as for you, ye thought evil against me; but God meant it unto good". (Genesis 50:20).**

A young man by the name of Barry Pittman was already a member of St. John and had been for years as well as the director of the Youth Choir.

It was Barry's idea to change the name of the choir from the Youth Choir to the Townsend Ensemble.

When it came to music and directing the choir, he took it very seriously. Barry knew music and he was a no nonesense director. During rehearsals, we were not leaving until he was satisfied that every note was sung correctly.

I remained president of the Townsends for seven years at which time I answered the call on my life to preach the gospel. During the time of my being the president was the time that the choir grew to almost a hundred members. As large as we were, the love for one another was still there. We were one big happy and blessed family. We enjoyed singing and worshiping together.

Into my seventh year as president, the choir was hit with some very unbelievable and disturbing news that rocked us to the core.

It was on March 11, 1995, that while the women were on a Women's Retreat in Scroons Lake, NY with Women on The Move we received the disturbing news that Barry our Director had passed. We were in service and at the time of getting this news his aunt Joyce was singing Order My Steps.

This was a tremendous loss for us, and we needed God more than ever before to comfort us and to ease the pain that felt like somebody had just stabbed us in our hearts.

Barry was only 29 years old when he passed from a Massive heart attack at home. He was so loved by the choir and he would always be there for you whenever you needed him.

Barry always made a fashion statement whenever he would dress. Dressing is what he loved to do and could do. He also loved to cook and travel. He did quite a bit of traveling because of the numerous choirs he belonged to. One being The Barbara Ward Farmer and The Wagner Alumni Choir as well as The Camden Community Choir just to name a few.

Upon our return home from the retreat, all I could think about was how are the Townsend's handling Barry's passing. A lot of them were around his age and close friends with him. Some of them grew up with him.

Once I got back, quite a few of them approached me in tears sharing with me that they couldn't cope with Barry's passing, and for a lot of them this was their first time going through the loss of someone close to them in age not to mention that he was a childhood friend to a lot of them.

As their president, and because I was approached by some of them, I knew the only thing I could do was to sincerely go to God in prayer seeking direction from Him as to what it was I could do to help the choir get through this ordeal.

Coming Out Of The Box!

On that coming Tuesday, the Townsends had choir rehearsal and it was then when I saw the faces of a group of broken-hearted, hurting not to mention grieving young people, that I realized I had to do what I was instructed to do in prayer.

What the Holy Spirit directed me to do meant I had to come out of the box, out of my comfort zone and most importantly be obedient to the will of the Father no matter the cost.

There is a song that is part of my testimony sung at my church lead by my dear sister-friend Deaconess Ana Pegram and the Voices of Faith Choir that I often direct called: "I 'Really' Love the Lord".

This song blesses my soul every time I hear it because I 'really' do love Him because folks don't know what He's done for me, He's made a way out of no way for me and He's given me the victory. I love Him for those reasons and more so I'm going to show Him just how much I love Him by being obedient to whatever it is He directs me to do. For the word of God lets us know that obedience is better than sacrifice: **"And Samuel said, Hath the Lord as great delight in burnt offerings and** sacrifices, as in obeying the voice of the Lord? Behold, to obey is better than sacrifice, and to hearken than the fat of rams." (1st Samuel 15:22").

While I was praying to God for direction, I could feel the Holy Spirit turning the crank on the box that I was crammed and stuffed in letting me know that it was time to be released from fear, time to be set free to do what I heard the voice of the Lord saying to me. It was time to come out of a box that God never intended for me or any of us to be in.

The instructions that I received from the Lord in prayer was to not have rehearsal but to anoint each member with oil and pray for them individually. My first thought was there are almost a hundred members and Lord you want me to do what? But isn't that just like us though? We ask God for direction and when He directs us in what it is He's directing us to do, we want to debate and question Him on His directions.

The next thought I had was anointing with oil was something that I had never seen being done in our church. Then the final thought and question I had was what would Pastor say?

I had all of these questions, doubts, and hesitations of doing what was told to me by the Holy Spirit, but with all of the questions, doubts, hesitation, and fear I had, the Lord knew me well enough to know that I would come out of that box being obedient and doing what He instructed me to do even when I had to do it afraid.

The one thing that I struggled with the most, was that I was not led to check with my Pastor about what the Holy Spirit had directed me to do.

Without question, I have the utmost respect for my pastor and there would be nothing I would do without seeking his guidance. There would be nothing I would do without talking to him first before making a move, but when I prayed for direction at such a crucial time, I knew that what I heard the Spirit say was coming directly from Him.

God was turning the crank on that box that I was in, but once the music stopped playing I just popped out of that box remaining focused on what the Lord's plans were for me to do for the choir.

There was no disrespect intended towards my pastor, but if nothing else, I knew that the Lord knew me well enough to trust me with such a mission and that my Pastor knew me well enough to know that I would only make a move like that because I had heard from the Lord.

I consider myself to be one of God's sheep that listens when He speaks and when He speaks to me I give Him my undivided attention so that I might hear Him clearly and distinctly.

When I'm praying and talking to my God there is no room for distractions. I need to be focused solely on what I have to say to Him as well as listening to what He has to say to me. **"My sheep hear my voice, and I know them, and they follow me" (John10:27).**

I am one who takes the word of God literally. Meaning, if He said it, then I not only believe it but I receive it. If He instructs me, then I am going to do it and if He sends me then I will go. Just like God knows me I know Him well enough to know that whatever He does in me, with me, and through me, I trust Him with my whole heart and I have complete faith in Him to know that He won't take me anywhere or let me do anything that His grace and mercy won't keep me.

We must learn to trust God in everything and with everything because He will not set us up to fail.

Putting our lives in His hands completely is saying that we know that He knows what is best for us. Yes! The Father knows best.

When we all gathered for choir rehearsal that Tuesday, we opened up in prayer. I started by talking about Barry's passing and how many of them came to me not knowing how to handle his death.

I further explained to them how heavy it was on my heart, that I didn't know what to say or do to try to comfort all of you. I was concerned about how his passing was affecting each one of you, so I did what I would normally do in any other situation and I took it to the Lord in prayer.

I needed to hear some instructions from Him that would help me to help you get through this terrible ordeal.

I talked, and He listened, He talked and I listened. What the Spirit instructed me to do was to anoint each of you and pray over you individually. In sharing that with them, I explained to them, that no one should feel obligated to stay nor did anyone have to feel they were being made or forced to have me lay hands and anoint them.

I told them that there would not be any rehearsal and that they could stay or leave at their discretion.

After sharing all that with them much to my surprise every single one of them remained and every one of them was open to receive what the Lord instructed me to do.

While anointing and praying over everyone I noticed that two Deacons were standing in the back of the fellowship hall and then they disappeared.

It wasn't long after they left, that Pastor rushed up into the fellowship hall, saw what I was doing, stood there for a few minutes turned around left out of the fellowship hall taking the two deacons with him.

I don't' know what those two Deacons said to him to make him rush in the way he did, but it became quite clear to me that whatever they said it wasn't enough for him to stop me from doing what I know the Holy Spirit told me to do.

When I finished praying for everyone, some of them came to me and we embraced while they shared with me how grateful they were for the prayer.

I was the last one to leave and as I was gathering up my things those same two Deacons came back into the fellowship hall and it was then that I felt for sure that I was going to be reprimanded. I just knew for sure that Pastor had sent them to tell me he wanted to see me, but that was not the case at all.

The pastor did send them back but He sent them back to pray for me. Yes, he sent them to do what I so desperately needed which was prayer! After individually praying for and anointing almost one hundred choir members I was not only physically but spiritually drained.

I thank God for turning the crank on the box that I found myself in. He kept turning the crank so to let me out to do what He had instructed me to do. I thank Him for a Pastor who knew me well enough to know that there is nothing I would do that would go against the will of God, the word of God, and without praying and seeking God's guidance and direction.

So many of us are like a Jack-In-The-Box waiting for a man to turn the crank to let us out not understanding that he doesn't want to let us out. He wants us to remain stuck in our past, stuck in our emotions, stuck by what other people think, say, and do. He wants to keep us in his clutches to keep the fear, doubt, frustration, and lack of trust in the one who is ready and willing to let us out of the box. As soon as the adversary lets us out and gives us the opportunity to get a taste of what it is like to be free, he quickly pushes us back down into that box. But the word of God says: **"Therefore if the Son makes you free, ye shall be free indeed" (John 8:36).**

It was when I had a heart to heart talk with my Pastor about how I was doing things that seem so strange to me and that's when he told me that I was out of the box and I'm so grateful for being set free and not entangled by the adversary any longer.

We must understand that boxes were made to hold items and to contain things not to contain God's children making them feel like a Jack-In-The-Box being afraid to move where and when God wants us to move, doing what He instructs us to do, and waiting for the enemy to turn the crank on the box to let us out.

The time is now that we must come out of the box of fear, doubt, anxiety, uncertainty and do whatever it is God is instructing us to do, trusting and believing by faith that He will see us through.

It is time now for us to put the enemy on notice and let him know that you are no longer his Jack-In-The-Box and that you have been set free from fear, doubt, and from being stuck in your past. Let him know that you know the truth of God's word and the truth has set you free.

PRAYER OF STRENGTH...

Lord God, I come thanking you for the opportunity of
coming out of the box so as to be and to do
all that you have planned for my life.
I thank you that I no longer feel pressured or influenced
by the lies and tactics of the adversary.
Thank you for breaking the chains off of me that had me so bound
and for giving me the strength to persevere no matter what.
Fear and doubt no longer had me bound. I
am free! In Jesus name – Amen!

SONG OF ENCOURAGEMENT
I REALLY LOVE THE LORD

I really love the Lord
I really love the Lord.
You don't know what He's done for me,
He gave me the victory
I love Him, I love Him
I really love the Lord.

Anybody here who loves my Jesus?
Anybody, anybody in here who loves who just loves the Lord?
Anybody here who loves my Jesus
I want to know, I want to know if you love the Lord?

Is there anybody here whom the Lord has made a way for?
And when it got dark in your life did the Lord brighten up your way?
You ought to wave your hand, you ought to shout for joy, if you really
love Jesus.
I want to know, I want to know if you love the Lord?

By: Rev. Charles Nicks Jr.& The Saints James Choir

5

"I'm Grateful"

Giving thanks always for all things unto God and the Father in the name of our Lord Jesus Christ.

EPHESIANS 5:20 KJV

We are living in a world whereby people do not seem to be grateful for anything. They walk around with an attitude as if the world owes them something. They have an attitude of entitlement, always looking to receive rather than to give.

No matter how much you do for them, seemingly it is never enough. You can bend over backward for people and they still do not appreciate what you do. It is almost like what you do for them is expected of you and sadly enough, that's how we treat God.

We expect Him to keep doing and doing, giving and giving to us while we keep taking and taking with no regards as to what we are to give Him in return nor do we show or tell Him just how grateful we are to him for all that He has already done.

Truth be told God does not owe us anything. He gave us His very best, which was His only begotten Son, and His Son gave us His best which was His life by dying a mean cruel death on Calvary. He died a death that paid a debt that we could not pay. **"For God so loved the world that He gave His only begotten Son, that whosoever believeth in Him should not perish, but have everlasting life." (John 3:16)**

The debt that He paid reminds me so much of that great hymn of the church that says: "Jesus paid it all, all to Him I owe. Sin had left a crimson stain, He washed it white as snow".

God has done so much for all of us that there should never be a minute or a second that goes by that we do not thank Him. We all I am sure can attest to the fact that no matter how many times we messed up God blessed us anyhow. Knowing that we were not deserving of the many blessings bestowed upon us, He still blessed us, which shows us just how deep His love is for us.

Some of us are seemingly too busy for God, but how ironic it is, that the things we busy ourselves with, are the things God blessed us with.

That job you have God blessed you with it! The children that you have God blessed you with them! Those grandchildren you lived long enough to see, He blessed you with them! Not to mention good health and strength, a roof over your head, food on your table and that list goes on and on.

We often misplace our priorities, not doing what we are instructed to do according to the word of God. The word of God tells us to: **"Seek ye first the kingdom of God, and His righteousness; and all these things shall be added unto you" (Matthew 6:33).**

Even when we put all those things ahead of God and never say or show Him just how grateful we are for them, He still loves us and will continually be there for us, watching over us, providing for us, and healing us because of the unconditional love He has for us.

God is so good and merciful towards us that we can't help but be grateful. How sad it is that we take God and the things He does for us for granted and we never say thank you. He has brought us all from a mighty long way. He's brought us through some hard times, painful and hurtful times, times when our finances were low, times when we were grieving, times when folks talked about us and did us wrong and we never thanked Him nor did we let Him know how truly grateful we were to Him on how He was there with us and for us.

There were times when we were sinking into that slimy, messy, muddy pit, but the Lord lifted us out of the muck and miry clay and He placed our feet on a firm foundation. **"He brought me up also out of an horrible pit, out of the miry clay, and set my feet upon a rock, and established my goings" (Psalm 40:2)**

God has constantly made a way out of no way for each of us more times than we deserve. He rescued us from dangers seen and unseen which most of the time we brought on ourselves. Every ordeal we have ever been through we came out of it because God alone made a way. **"Behold, I will do a new thing; now it shall spring forth; shall ye not know it? I will even make a way in the wilderness, And rivers in the desert." (Isaiah 43:19).** Jesus is always in the business of making ways out of no way.

When the God we serve makes a way out of no way for us, giants they do fall! Jericho walls they do come down! Lions will get locked jaw! the red sea will open up in front of us and pharaoh's army who is behind us will drown because they can't swim! Blinded eyes will open, storms will cease, the sick are healed, the addicted are delivered, liars will stop lying and the unsaved are saved. Who would not want to be grateful and thankful to and for a God like this?

We all have a story to tell about how God made a way out of no way and how He saved you from the clutches of the adversary. Stories about how death might have crept up into your room but mercy said no and God held back the night. Stories about how you may have been strung out on drugs and you may have felt that if God did not intervene on your behalf you weren't going to make it but then there was light at the end of that tunnel and God delivered you from your addiction. **"Many are the afflictions of the righteous: But the Lord delivereth him out of them all" (Psalm 34:19).**

The word of God says: **"O taste and see that the Lord is good: Blessed is the man that trusteth in Him" (Psalm 34:8).** As for me, I have many stories and testimony's that I could tell about how I tasted of God's goodness towards me but the one that resonates in my spirit at this moment is the most recent one which happened to me two years ago.

It's a testimony as to how God will show us just how good He is when we completely put our full trust in Him no matter what the circumstances or how bad the situation may look.

My Testimony!

It was on a Wednesday morning, November 7, 2018, when I experienced something I never experienced before in my life. It was a scary moment and the only name I knew to call on was the name of Jesus.

I got up that morning with the plans of going to see my mother who was in rehab. I got up, took a shower, and then got dressed.

I then went back into the bathroom to brush my teeth and it was then that I got a really bad pain on the right side of my head just above my eye.

It was so painful I had to stop doing what I was doing. It paralyzed me to the point of just standing still holding onto the sink. Then suddenly the bathroom started spinning around and I felt like I was going to pass out.

Slowly I grabbed hold to the door and then the wall, asking God, please help me get back to my room so that I could sit down in my chair.

I had to go down the hallway to my room, which isn't long at all, but at that moment it felt like a lifetime to get there but with the Lord's help, I made it to the chair.

I began feeling so weak and nauseous and I knew I had to call someone and the only person I knew to call was my brother Stump who happened to live only two doors down from me.

I had a landline phone in my room on my nightstand near where I was sitting, but I did not know my brother's number. When I was growing up all we had was a landline phone, a time when we had to memorize phone numbers but today when we have cell phones all we have to do is pull up the name and the number would be right there.

I began to panic because I had to reach him. On my bed were bibles, a laptop, and papers, but amidst all of those things I heard the Holy Spirit say, look closer on the bed and low and behold, there was my cell phone. No one can never tell me that the Lord was not in the midst of my situation because normally my phone would be downstairs charging and I clearly don't remember bringing my phone upstairs much less putting it on my bed.

The thoughts I had when I picked up the phone was that I did not have the strength nor the energy to look for much less dial his number.

Then again, the Holy Spirit spoke to me and said, hit the call log and when I did my brother's name was at the top and all I needed to do was hit his name and his number popped right up. God already knew what I was going to need before I even asked Him. **"And it shall come to pass, that before they call, I will answer; and while they are yet speaking, I will hear"** (Isaiah 65:24).

I got my brother on the phone and told him I needed him to come right over because something was going on with me that I could not explain.

The blessing in getting him when I did was that I caught him as he was going to his car to go take his walk around Cooper River. If I had tried to go down the stairs, which I could not do, to get my phone I would have missed him and probably fallen down the steps. But God! My phone was right there on my bed with his name at the top of the call log. As soon as I hung the phone up from him I heard the Holy Spirit say call Joann.

Now make no mistake about it, I love my sister but going through what I was going through, dealing with the pain in my head and vertigo, Minister Joann Cade was the last person on my mind to call but God knew who and what I needed. Now I am thinking, God I don't know her number either and again the Holy Spirit spoke and said the call log, and when I looked at my phone her name was the second name listed and I just hit the button.

When she answered, she asked how I was doing and with her medical background and hearing how I was sounding she told me to hang up and call 911 because I didn't' sound right to her. As soon as I hung up my brother was coming up the steps and by this time I felt like I was passing out.

When he came into my room, I can remember my head being down but I was able to lift it up long enough to tell him to call 911. After that, I must have passed out because the next thing I remember there were about six paramedics in my room and these guys were big. I felt like I was surrounded by God's heavenly angels.

With my head still hanging down, one of the paramedics attending to me was taking my blood pressure and while he was doing that, a man crawled across my bed. I couldn't speak but in my mind, I was saying who is this man crawling across my bed with his shoes on? Come to find out he was a Doctor. He reached out to grab my hand and said, "Mrs. Moore don't worry, you're going to be alright". At that time I felt like it was God speaking through this man consoling me and reassuring me that everything was going to be alright.

It was not long after that the doctor consoled me that the paramedic who was taking my blood pressure said let's get her out of here her blood pressure is 180/189. They put me in a chair and those six men carried me down the steps to the ambulance.

Once I got to the hospital, I felt worst. I was getting more nauseous and could not stop throwing up. It got to the point when nothing was coming up and I ended up having the dry heaves.

The emergency room they had me in was constantly spinning and after being thoroughly examined it was told to me and my family that I had a stroke and a very bad case of Vertigo and that they had to admit me.

I was admitted to Cooper Hospital and was there for seven days. Once I left the hospital I was taken to Kessler Rehabilitation of which I stayed about a month.

While there, I went through physical therapy, and occupational therapy. The stroke affected my eyesight to the point that I was not seeing clearly. I had to wear a patch over each eye switching them every day.

I had therapy every morning and was looking forward to it until this one particular morning I started getting symptoms very similar to the ones I had when I first had the stroke.

The room was spinning around and I felt nauseous again. I did not have the energy to get out the bed much less go to therapy and my vision seemingly had gotten worst.

I was getting pain on the same side of my head and in the same spot. All I could think about was Lord please do not let me have another stroke. I was told that it would not take much for me to have another one.

The therapist came to my room to get me for therapy but I told her I could not do it today and that I was not feeling well. She asked me, what was wrong? I told her my symptoms and I was especially feeling nauseous. She told me that they would check back with me later. One thing I found out about Kessler is that they do not let you skip therapy so easily.

They came back to my room at least two more times and I still was feeling terrible. I figured since it was late in the afternoon that they would not come back and that I would be able to stay in the bed and rest. But I thought wrong because here they come again for the third time and by now I was getting a little agitated so I told them I see you're not going to give up so I'm going to try to get up and go.

The whole time I went through therapy I always had a woman but when I went to the therapy room this time, I had a young man by the name of Brian. He approached me and asked me my name and he told me his. He then began to strike up a conversation with me asking me what happened to me and I told him I had a stroke. He asked me was I told the type of stroke I had and I told him no, that I was only told that I had a stroke.

It was at this point and time that I began to think about how intentional God is. What are the odds that the day I was having all of those reoccurring symptoms that would be the day that Brian would be there to give me not only therapy but, he gave me information regarding my stroke that I had no knowledge of. I would not have known the type of stroke I had, had Brian not been there. I can only thank God for His presence with me throughout this whole ordeal.

Brian asked me did I know what type of stroke I had and I said no. He shared with me that the type of stroke I had was called a Medulla and that it was the worst type of stroke one could have.

He explained to me that the Medulla is located at the back and the lower region of the brain, connected to the spinal cord.

It is responsible for regulating functions of the autonomic nervous

system, including respiration, cardiac function, vasodilation, and re-
flexes like vomiting, coughing, sneezing, and swallowing.

He then asked me if I knew the statistics of the Medulla stroke
and I told him no. He then proceeded to tell me that 33% get through
it with therapy but they still have some symptoms to deal with – 33%
end up being paralyzed and then the last 33% they die. He then said
that I was very lucky but after hearing those statistics, my response to
him was no, I'm not lucky, luck has nothing to do with how the Lord
kept me, I'm blessed and highly favored.

I thanked him for all the information that he gave me and when I
got back to my room I started processing everything he told me and
then I couldn't' do anything else but praise my God.

I praised Him and thanked Him for how He kept me during my
whole situation. He did not have to do what He did for me but He
did and I am so grateful. He didn't have to let my phone be on my
bed but He did, He didn't have to let my brother be there but He did,
He didn't have to tell me to call Joann but He did, He didn't have to
keep me from falling into the statistics giving me but He did and I
am truly grateful.

As I laid there in my bed I kept thinking over and over again
about everything Brian told me but it was something about those
statistics that made me realize that God is truly the keeper I've
known Him to be. It was something about the 33% that got me to
thinking.

I began saying wow God, 33% go through therapy and they still
have symptoms they have to contend with. The next 33% are paralyzed and then there is the 33% which die. My thoughts were God
that is only 99% so what about the 1% and He spoke to my spirit ever
so clearly, that you Jackie are the 1%. You are the 1% that did not fall
into any of the percentages given.

Many patients were coming and going into therapy and you were the only one who thanked me even when you were yet going through. Even when Brian told you that you were lucky you did not hesitate to let him know that luck had nothing to do with your situation and that you were blessed. You are that one percent that I know will go back and tell others about My keeping power and how grateful you are. You are that one percent who will make sure that I get all the glory, honor, and praise, and that my glory will be revealed.

When I heard that in my spirit about being the only one who thanked Jesus I reflected on a message I preached about the ten lepers entitled "I'm the Grateful One" **(Luke 17:11-19)**.

It was when Jesus went to Jerusalem, and He passed through Samaria and Galilee and as He entered into a certain village, He met ten men that were lepers. They stood off in the distance and cried out Jesus, Master, have mercy on us. Jesus told them to go show themselves to the priest and while they were on their way, they were healed. Out of the ten, one of them saw that he was healed and he was the only one who came back to thank Him.

When he came back Jesus asked were there not ten of you where are the other nine? Are you the only one who came back to give me praise? He then told the man which was a Samaritan to rise and go his way for his faith has made him whole.

Just like that Samaritan who was the only one to come back and thank Jesus for his healing, I too am the only one that one percent who told Jesus thank you and showed Him just how grateful I am.

Grateful for how He's kept me, protected me, covered me, provided for me, healed me, delivered me, blessed me, loves me, directs me, instructs me, and ever so grateful to Him for saving me.

I might not have seen it or understood it back then when I went through the split of my home church or even the six years I spent at the church I now call my healing station, but one thing I do know is that I am grateful to God for where He brought me from to where He's brought me to. I'm grateful for where He has me in my life today. I am grateful for the many trials He brought me through because they made me strong. I am grateful for all the people He has in my life who have been there praying for me as well as for my family.

I am always going to be grateful to my heavenly Father for everything He allows me to face and go through in life because I know Him well enough to know that He will be there with me and for me every step of the way.

I can stand on His promise that lets me know **"I will never leave thee, nor forsake thee" (Hebrews 15:5b)** .

If God can't depend on anyone else to thank Him and be grateful for all that He has done for them, He knows for sure He can always count on me to be that grateful one, that one percent who will always come back and say thank YOU.

With life's trials, challenges, trouble, and problems that we all face, satan the adversary will always try to do evil against us by creating fear in us, distracting us, discouraging us, persecuting us, causing us to doubt and question God. But when those times come and we can't trace His hand we can always trust His plan. satan has been and will continue to be a defeated foe, and because he will, you can look him right in the eye and tell him what the word of God says which is: **"But as for you, ye thought evil against me; but God meant it unto good, to bring to pass, as it is this day, to save much people alive." (Genesis 50:20)** .

In everything that we go through in life that does not seem to be working out for our good that is the time to shout "BUT GOD" and that will be our shout of hope that God is working it all out for our good.

PRAYER OF GRATEFULNESS

Father in the name of Jesus, I come thanking and praising
You for all that You have done for me. I thank you for
experiencing your healing touch. I thank you for being there
for me in the worst of times. I'm so grateful to you and I know
for myself, there's no one like you Jesus, and can't nobody do for me
what you continuously do for me and that's why I will
continue to be that one percent that shows you just how
grateful I truly am. In Jesus name, I pray Amen!

SONG OF ENCOURAGEMENT
"GRATEFUL"

I am
Grateful for the things
That you have done
Yes, I'm grateful for the victories we've won
I could go on and on and on
About your works
Because I'm grateful, grateful, grateful
Just to praise you Lord
Flowing from my heart
Are the issues of my heart
It's gratefulness

Song by: Hezekiah Walker and The Love Fellowship Choir

Epilogue

A Final Word

God never promised that once we receive Jesus Christ as our Lord and Savior, that life for us as a born again believer would be without pain, hurt, difficulty, trials struggles, and trouble.

With all of the many promises God has made to us in His word, being exempt from trouble was not one of them. However, He did promise that when faced with or going through hard and difficult times that: **"Lo I am with you always, even unto the end of the world" (Matthew 28:20).** He did promise: "I will never leave you nor forsake you" He did promise that: He would be a very present help in the time of trouble" and this is just a few of the numerous promises made to the children of God.

Not everything that happens to us in life is going to be a bed of roses and there will be times when circumstances will not look good, feel good, be good, or have a good outcome.

Every morning that we are blessed to wake up is not necessarily going to be a good morning! Every day that we tunnel through is not going to be a good day! And there is no guarantee that every night is going to be a restful and peaceful night.

Moreover, there is no question or doubt, that we are beyond blessed when we can open our eyes to see a brand new morning.

When we can make it through another day's journey we are extremely blessed. Yes, we are blessed, blessed, blessed when God decides to hold back the night, not letting death creep up in our room.

However, "stuff still happens". In the morning when we rise, "stuff happens," during the day as we are going about our daily routine, "stuff happens", even when we're sleeping, "stuff is happening.

Unfortunately, the trials, temptations, problems, and troubles of this world are not put on hold because we are saved, but thank God for Jesus, that we have a Savior who when the stuff does happen in our lives He never slumbers nor sleeps: **"Behold, he that keepeth Israel shall neither slumber nor sleep" (Psalm 121:4).**

We have a God who is "Omniscient", one who knows everything there is to know about what we are going through. He's "Omnipresent" one who is present everywhere at the same time taking care of business for us; He's "Omnipotent", one who has unlimited power and is able to do anything but fail not to mention that He is our Sovereign Lord. No one dictates to Him what to do, how to do it, and how to go about doing it. He does what He wants, when and how He wants.

This is the one and only true God in whom we can always have faith and trust in. The one of whom we can rely and depend on with full trust and confidence to not only see us through it all but who is able and willing to bring us out of it all.

We've got to believe that He can handle it and that whatever our "It" is in life, God's got "It" and He's got you in the midst of it all. No matter how often trouble presents itself at your front door, know that as long as you turn it all over to Him, trust Him with it all and rest in Him through it all, you will unequivocally understand that our God is able. **"Now unto him, that is able to do exceeding abundantly above all that we ask or think, according to the power that worketh in us." (Ephesians 3:20).**

It is then that you will see and know at His appointed time, that

"All Things work together for the good of them that love God, to them who are the called according to his purpose." (Romans 8:28).

No matter what good, bad, or ugly experiences and or challenges transpire in our lives, undoubtedly, they all have a purpose in the will, and plan of God for us all. "For I know the thoughts that I think toward you, saith the Lord, thoughts of peace, and not of evil, to give you an expected end" (Jeremiah 29:11). Not to mention that the things in and of this world are temporary and that those experiences and or challenges also have an expiration date. "For our light affliction which is but for a moment, worketh for us a far more exceeding and eternal weight of glory;"(2nd Corinthians 4:17).

God is in the business of turning your situations around. He can turn your midnight into day; and your mourning into morning. "Weeping may endure for a night but joy cometh in the morning" (Psalm 30:5).

Knowing that God is in full control of everything that involves and concerns us and knowing that He is able to do what only He and no one else can do, it will help us to draw closer to Him and He to us. "Draw nigh to God, and he will draw nigh to you... (James 4:8a).

The closer we get to God, we will experience such a craving for His word and His presence like never before. We will have a thirst for Him that is unquenchable. A thirst that can only be quenched by the living water which is the word of God. "As the deer panteth after the water brooks so panteth my soul after thee oh God" (Psalm 42:1).

It is only through the reading, studying, meditating, believing, trusting, and applying God's word that we can and will ever experience true hope, love, and victory during our time of trouble. "But his delight is in the law of the Lord; and in his law doth he meditate day and night" (Psalm 1:2) "Study to show thyself approved unto God, a workman

that needeth not to be ashamed, rightly dividing the word of truth"
(2ⁿᵈ Timothy 2:15)

The word of God is powerful, and it is also liberating. It is the inerrant, infallible word of God, which has, is and always will be the only true source that we will ever need to get us through anything. It will help us face anything and give us the strength to fear nothing and no one! **"The Lord is my light and my salvation, whom shall I fear? The Lord is the strength of my life; of whom shall I be afraid?" (Psalm 27:1).**

For so long we have been putting God on the back burner when going through. We call on our friends before we call on God; we trust in our resources before we trust in God, and we seek status and position before we seek God. **(Matthew 6:33)** makes it not only clear, but it gives us order as to what should come first in the Kingdom of God. **"But seek ye first the kingdom of God, and his righteousness, and all these things shall be added unto you".**

It is so imperative, that we seek God first in everything, particularly during our troublesome times trusting that He's got the situation under control and He's not going to allow satan to defeat you no matter what it looks like.

God never fails to bless us, answer our prayers, provide for us, protect us and keep us, so we must always keep our priorities straight and not only put Him first but keep Him first in all that we do. It is time for us to stop taking Him for granted and treating Him as if He's a part-time lover. God has so many blessings stored up for us we just have to put Him first, trust and have faith in Him and believe that He will do what needs to be done in His timing,

In conclusion, there ought not to be anything keeping us from boldly opening up our mouths to say, "HALLELUJAH ANYHOW", which is that ray of hope, that reminds us that because we are still here and in our right mind it is quite evident that "HE'S A KEEPER" and that when we pray the "PRAYER OF FAITH", it removes all of our doubts and fears that had us bound and God is faithful in answering our prayers that sets us free to come "OUT OF THE BOX" and for that "I AM GRATEFUL".

Nothing remains the same "BUT GOD!!!".

BUT GOD

By grace I was saved,
Because of Him who rose from the grave,
Not a deed that we've done,
To deserve the gift of His Son,
Yes, I know where I would be
If He had not died for me,

See some of you were liars, But God, but God
Some of you were haters, But God, But Bod
See some of you were deceivers, But God, But God
If it's the road of bondage and sin that you trod
Don't give up, so did I, but God.

So trust what I say,
For tonight you can receive His love today.
If you're here and you're lost,
Know that Jesus paid the cost,
At the cross between two theives,
Ask of Him, Lord remember me.

Now some of you were backbiters, But God
Some of you were murders, But God, But God
Some of you were street walkers, But God, But God
If it's the road of bondage and sin that you trod
Don't give up, so did I, But God.

Yes, I was (I was lost in sin),
But He changed me,
That I might, I would soon reach,
(to reach the price, I'm gonna press ahead)
(and I'm grateful).

But God, but God,
But God, but God,
But God, but God
If It's the road of bondage and sin that you trod

Don't give up.
Don't give up.
Don't give up
So did I, but God.

Song by: Ron Winans
Found on website

But God Scriptures

Genesis 8:1	Acts 2:24
Genesis 31:7	Acts 3:15
Genesis 31:23-24	Acts 10:28
Genesis 31:42	Acts 13:29-30
Deuteronomy 7:7-8	Roman 5:8
1st Samuel 23:4	Romans 6:23
1st Kings 5:4	1st Corinthians 2:10
2nd Chronicles 20:15	1st Corinthians 3:6
Psalm 73:26	1st Corinthians 10:13
Psalm 86:15	1st Corinthians 1:27
Hosea 1:7	Galatians 1:15-16
Jonah 2:6	Galatians 3:18
Matthew 19:26	2nd Timothy 2:9
John 1:18	Ephesian 2:1, 3,4-5

Made in the USA
Middletown, DE
19 March 2021